Diner Mighty books can be made available at discount rates for volume purchases. We can work with you to customize this book or create unique books for your brand.

For details, write to **info@dinermighty.com**

www.DinerMighty.com

 ©2019 Joe Lacey

All rights reserved. Apart from any fair dealing for the purpose of private study, research, criticism or review, as permitted under the Copyright Designs and Patents Act, 1988, no part of this publication may be reproduced, stored in a retrieval system, or transmitted in any form or by any means, electronic, electrical, chemical, mechanical, optical, photocopying, recording or otherwise, without the prior written consent of the copyright owner. Enquiries should be addressed to the Publishers. Every attempt has been made by the Publishers to secure the appropriate permissions for materials reproduced in this book. If there has been any oversight, we will be happy to rectify the situation and a written submission should be made to the Publishers.

Joe Lacey has asserted his right under the Copyright, Designs and Patents Act, 1988, to be identified as the author of this book.

Book design by Joe Lacey, Los Angeles, CA. Cover illustration ©Joe Lacey.

Published by Diner Mighty Graphics in 2019.

Diner Mighty Graphics and the DM graphics logo are trademarks of Diner Mighty. Alley Gator™ name, logo design, and character design are trademarks of Diner Mighty.

ISBN: 978-1-7339842-1-8

First Edition

The ALLEY GATOR™ Bowling Book

with **30 Score Sheets**
and **Scoring Instructions**

PLUS
- Types of rolls
- Glossary of terms
- Bowling etiquette
- Introductory rules
- Jokes, fun facts, & activities

DINER MIGHTY
GRAPHICS

PLAYING THE GAME

- A bowling game is made up of 10 frames. A frame is equal to one turn. The bowler tries to knock down as many pins as possible in a frame.

- If the bowler knocks down all ten pins on the first roll, then that frame is over.

- If the bowler misses all the pins or leaves some pins standing on the first roll, the bowler gets another roll.

- In the tenth frame, if all the pins are knocked down on the bowler's first or second roll, the bowler gets a **BONUS** roll.

TEN-PIN BOWLING

The most common type of bowling is ten-pin bowling. A bowler rolls a ball down the bowling lane toward ten pins that are set up at the end of the lane. The bowler tries to knock down all ten pins on the first roll. This is a **STRIKE**. If the bowler misses or knocks down less than ten pins, the bowler gets a second roll and tries to knock down the remaining pins. This is a **SPARE**.

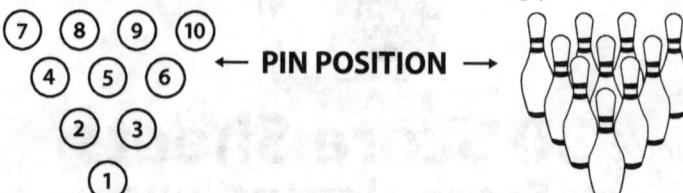

← PIN POSITION →

OTHER TYPES OF PIN BOWLING

Candlepin bowling
Candlepins are the tallest and thinnest pins, standing 15.75 inches tall. They have a slight taper at each end which makes them look like candles. Candlepin balls are 4.5 inches in diameter and weigh as much as 2 pounds 7 ounces. They have no finger holes and are the smallest of the three types of bowling balls.

Duckpin bowling
Duckpins are short, squatty pins, standing 9.4 inches tall. Duckpin balls are about 5 inches in diameter, the size of a softball, and weigh as much as 3 pounds 12 ounces. They have no finger holes. It is difficult to make a strike playing duckpin bowling, so the bowler is allowed three rolls per frame.

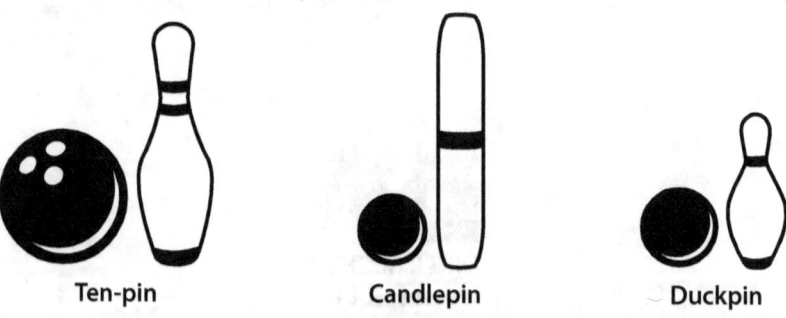

Ten-pin   Candlepin   Duckpin

BOWLING BALLS

 Bowling balls commonly weigh as little as 6 pounds as much as 16 pounds. They are 8.5 inches in diameter.

 Bowling balls have holes for your two fingers and thumb. Holding the ball is called the *grip*.

 Bowling balls can have as many as 12 holes! 5 holes can be used for gripping — one for each finger and thumb on one hand.

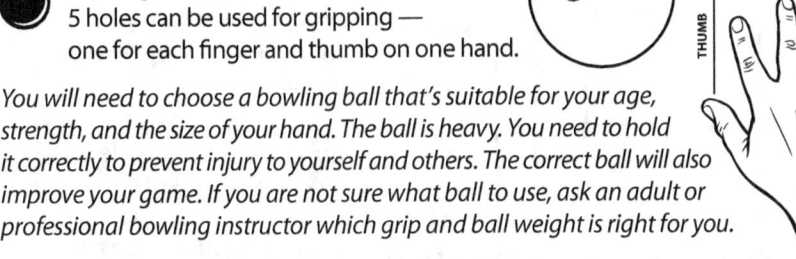

You will need to choose a bowling ball that's suitable for your age, strength, and the size of your hand. The ball is heavy. You need to hold it correctly to prevent injury to yourself and others. The correct ball will also improve your game. If you are not sure what ball to use, ask an adult or professional bowling instructor which grip and ball weight is right for you.

NOTE: A bowling glove helps support the wrist, improve grip, and prevent injuries.

BOWLING PINS

 Bowling pins are 4.75 inches wide at their widest point and 15 inches tall.

They can weigh 3 pounds 6 ounces or as much as 3 pounds 10 ounces.

Pins are often made from a very hard wood called "rock maple". Pins can also be made from synthetic materials. When struck by a bowling ball, wooden pins sound different than synthetic pins. Wooden pins have a brighter "cracking" sound than synthetic pins. Next time you are at a bowling alley, ask what kind of pins are used. Can you hear the difference?

BOWLING SHOES

 Most bowling alleys provide bowling shoes for you when you pay for a game. You are never allowed to wear your sneakers or "street shoes" while you bowl. Street shoes can damage the bowling lane.

 The soles of bowling shoes can be made of leather or microfiber. This makes them slide on the bowling lanes, giving the bowler a smoother motion. The heels of the shoes are rubber to help stop the bowler sliding after the ball is rolled.

Most bowling shoes are designed with one shoe for sliding and one shoe for braking. A right-handed player will have the sliding shoe on the left and a braking shoe on the right, and vice versa for a left-handed player. Sliding and braking shoes are often colored differently at the bowling alley to show which is which. Some bowling shoes come with interchangeable soles and heels.

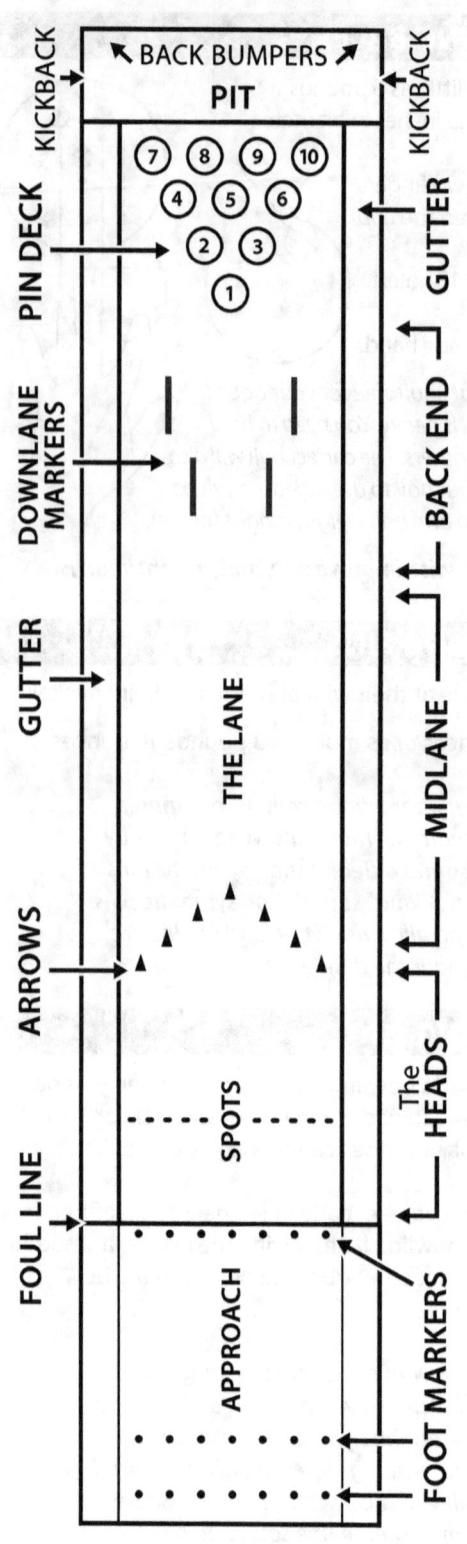

LANE BASICS

● Bowling lanes are 60 feet long from the foul line to the center of the head pin.

● The lane is 41.5 inches wide. At the front of the lane, there are two sets of dots 12 feet and 15 feet behind the foul line. They help with foot placement.

● The lane is made up of 39 boards of either wood or synthetic material. Each board is about one inch wide and can help with aiming and studying the ball's roll. Modern synthetic lanes may actually be a solid surface, but often have an overlay that resembles natural wood boards.

● If you are right-handed you will count the boards form left to right. If you are left-handed, you will count them right to left. The middle board is always number 20.

● It is considered best to keep your eyes on the arrows when beginning your approach. You should look at the pins *after* you have released the ball.

● An oiling machine is used to apply oil to the lane. The ball will change direction (hook) in areas that have less oil. The ball will not change direction (skid) in areas that have more oil. More oil decreases ball friction. Less oil increases ball friction.

THE BOWLING LANE

APPROACH — The area behind the foul line where the bowlers make their delivery.

ARROWS — Seven regularly-spaced arrowhead-shaped markers located about 15 feet past the foul line. They are used as guides or targets for rolling the ball.

BALL RETURN — An automated machine that moves the bowler's ball from the pit and sends it rolling back to the bowler on a ball return track.

BACK BUMPERS — Bumpers located behind the pit.

BUMPERS — Rails or barriers that surround a lane to prevent balls from going into the gutters. Bumpers are used mainly for beginners or young children.

DOWNLANE MARKERS — Two pairs of three-foot long guide lines beginning 34 and 40 feet past the foul line. They help bowlers see where their balls reach the breakpoint. Also called "rangefinders".

FOOT MARKERS — Two sets of dots behind the foul line to help with foot placement as the bowler prepares to bowl.

FOUL LINE — A line at the front of the lane which may not be crossed over.

GUTTER — One of two trough-shaped structures surrounding a lane to catch balls that roll off the lane. Also known formally as the "channel".

(The) HEADS — The front part of the lane, roughly from the foul line to the arrows.

MIDLANE — The part of the lane between the heads and the back end.

BACK END — The third of the lane furthest from the foul line.

INSIDE — If you are right-handed, the inside is the portion of the lane further to the left. If you are left-handed, the inside is the portion of the lane further to the right.

OUTSIDE — If you are right-handed, the outside is the portion of the lane further to the right. If you are left-handed, the outside is the portion of the lane further to the left.

KICKBACK — The walls outside the gutters that enclose the pin deck.

OIL — The lubricating conditioner applied to the front two-thirds of the lane.

PIN DECK — Area of the lane on which the pins stand, directly in front of the pit.

PIT — The area behind the pin deck that collects knocked over pins.

PAIR — Two lanes that share a common ball return.

SPOTS — A set of dots located about six feet beyond the foul line to help in aiming the ball.

SWEEP BAR — A mechanical bar that removes fallen and leftover pins from the pin deck area. Also known as a "rake bar".

TRACKS — Bowtie-shaped rings of oil from the lane left on a bowling ball after a shot.

THE FOUR BASIC SHOTS

STRAIGHT BALL — A bowling ball rolled slightly off-center, traveling along a straight line, and aimed at the first pin.

HOOK BALL — A bowling ball that rolls in a curve. The hook commonly scores more strikes than any other shot.

CURVE BALL — An extreme version of the hook ball, but with more room for error and it can be difficult to control.

BACKUP BALL — A hook ball that rolls in the opposite direction of a normal hook. *Example: When a ball is rolled by a right-hander, the ball hooks from left to right.*

THE THREE PHASES OF BALL MOTION

SKID — Phase 1: The ball travels a straight path until reaching the breakpoint.

HOOK — Phase 2: The ball begins to curve around the midlane.

ROLL — Phase 3: The ball reaches full traction and heads to the pins.

FORM

CRANKER — A bowler who releases the ball with high revolutions. This style favors power over control and repeatability.

STROKER — A bowler who releases the ball in a smooth and controlled manner.

TWEENER — A bowler whose style is somewhere between a *stroker* and *cranker*.

CLASSIC APPROACH

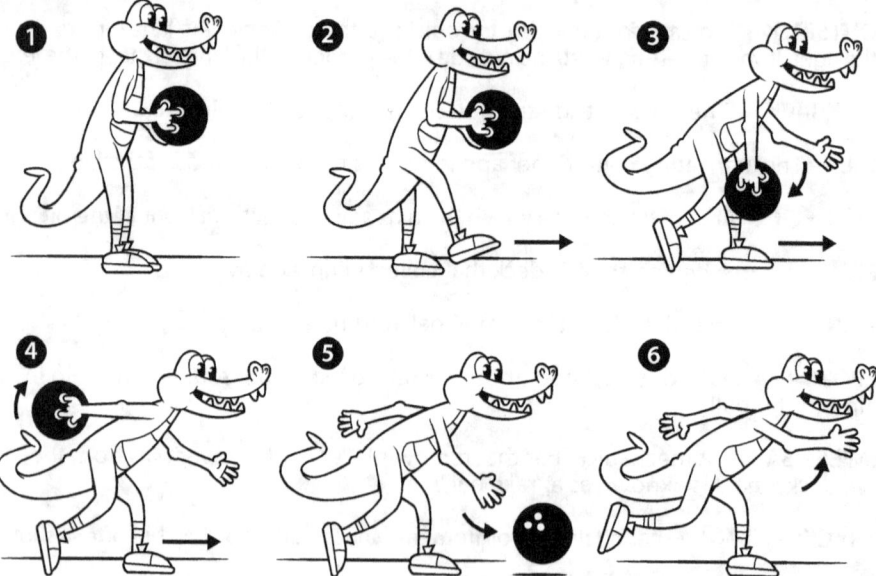

ROUNDS

TOURNAMENT — A contest among a large number of bowlers.

QUALIFYING ROUNDS — The beginning stage of a tournament. Bowlers compete to determine who will proceed to the match rounds.

MATCH ROUNDS — The intermediate stage of a tournament. Bowlers compete to determine their ranking for the final rounds.

FINAL ROUNDS — The last stage of a tournament. Also referred to as "finals".

STEPLADDER FINALS — One-on-one bowling matches in which the winner advances and the loser is out of the game.

BOWLING BALLS & BOWLERS

CORE — A dense structure inside a bowling ball that can be shaped and located to affect the ball's motion.

COVERSTOCK — The material that makes up a bowling ball's outer surface or cover.

DRILLING LAYOUT — This refers to where and how a ball's holes are drilled. Holes are drilled to accommodate a bowler's preferred grip.

GRIP — The manner in which the bowling ball is held.

    CONVENTIONAL GRIP — A ball grip in which the fingers are inserted to the second knuckle from the fingertips and the thumb is inserted completely.

    FINGERTIP GRIP — A ball grip in which the fingers are inserted only to the first knuckle from the fingertips while the thumb is inserted completely.

HOUSE BALL — A non-custom ball provided by bowling facilities for use by patrons.

KEGLER — A person who bowls.

SPAN — The distance between a ball's finger holes and the thumb hole.

PINS

DEAD WOOD — A pin left on the lane or in the gutter out of reach of the sweep bar.

HEAD PIN — Pin at the front of the triangular arrangement of bowling pins. *Pin #1.*

KING PIN — Pin that stands in the middle of the triangular arrangement of bowling pins. *Pin #5.*

MESSENGER — A pin that travels sideways across the pin deck, often knocking over other pins. Also known as a "bird dog", "scout", "shrapnel", or "rogue pin".

SLEEPER — A pin positioned directly behind another pin after the first ball roll.

STICK — Another word for pin.

TEN-PIN STYLE BOWLING PINS — The largest and heaviest pins in bowling.

TYPES OF ROLLS

AXIS OF ROTATION — The angle that the ball rotates as it travels down the lane.

BABY-SPLIT — A split in which both pins are hit with the ball. *Examples: 2-7, 3-10.*

BAGGER — A series of strikes in a row. *Examples: six-bagger, seven-bagger, etc.*

BACKDOOR STRIKE — A strike in which the ball misses the head pin, but then the head pin is knocked down by other pins.

BROOKLYN — A roll in which the ball crosses over the centerline to hit the pins on a side opposite of the pocket. Also known as a "Jersey" or "Windsor".

CHEESY CAKES — Strikes which are relatively easy. Also known as "cake shot".

CHICKEN — Three spares in a row. Also known as a "sparrow".

CHICKEN SANDWICH — Three spares in a row, preceded and followed by strikes. Example: *Strike • Spare • Spare • Spare • Strike.*

DOUBLE — Two strikes in a row.

EARLY TIMING — A delivery in which the ball is released before the sliding foot slides.

FIELD GOAL — A failed 7-10 split conversion attempt in which the ball goes between the two pins.

FLUSH — A full pocket hit usually resulting in sending all ten pins into the pit.

GOLDEN TURKEY — Nine strikes in a row.

HAMBONE — Four strikes in a row within one game. Also known as a "4-bagger".

MIXER — A roll that causes the pins to bounce around or "mix" extensively.

RIDE THE LIGHTNING — When a ball is rolled close to the gutter.

SPARE — Scoring result of 10 points in a frame in which the last of the ten pins are knocked down on the second roll of the frame.

SPLIT — A spare in which the head pin is knocked down but at least two non-adjacent pins remain standing with a gap between them. The 7-10 split is the hardest to roll.

SPINNER — A bowling ball which spins like a top when rolled.

STRIKE — Scoring result of 10 points in a frame in which all ten pins are knocked down on the first roll.

TURKEY — Three strikes in a row.

WALL SHOT — A strike in which pins bounce off the side walls.

WASHOUT — A leave in which the head pin and at least two non-adjacent pins remain standing.

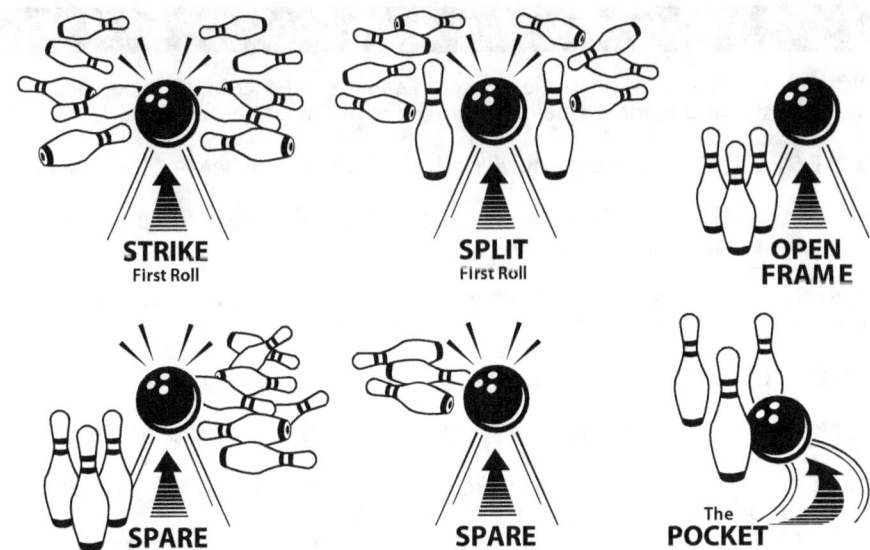

AXIS OF ROTATION

Top view, ball moves forward while at the same time rotating on its axis. At 0°, the ball rolls forward with no axis rotation. At 30° and 60°, the ball moves forward and at the same time rotates on its axis.

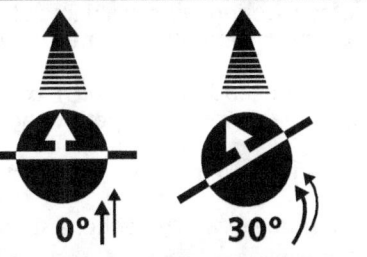

SPARES

Black circles indicate pins left standing.

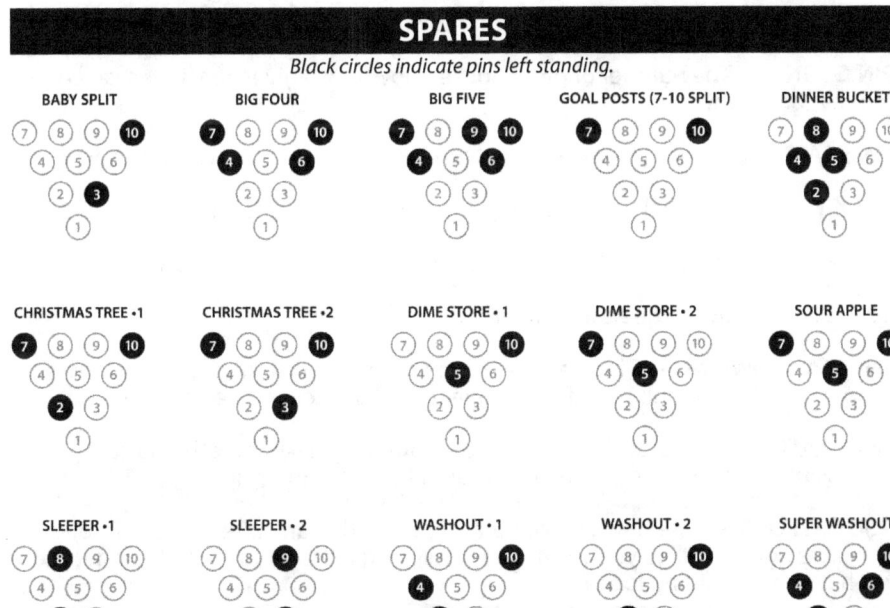

GAME PLAY & SCORING

ANCHOR — When bowling in a league or in a team, the anchor is the person bowling last. The anchor is usually the bowler with the highest average.

ANGLE OF ENTRY — The angle at which the ball is moving when first hitting a pin.

APPROACH — The part of the delivery that leads up to the release. *Approach* is also the name of the area behind the foul line.

AVERAGE — The total of scores from multiple games divided by the number of games. The average is rounded down to a whole-number value.

AUTOMATIC SCORER — A computerized scoring system used in modern bowling.

BREAKPOINT — The location where the ball begins to turn toward the *pocket*.

DELIVERY — The process a bowler takes when rolling a bowling ball. It begins with the approach and ends with the release of the ball.

FOUL — The bowler's swing arm goes over the foul line or the bowler's foot touches or slides over the foul line (foot foul). The bowler receives zero points.

FRAME — One of ten scoring units in a game of bowling. Each frame includes one or two rolls (two or three in the 10th frame) depending on the pin count.

HANDICAP — A number added to a *scratch score*. Often given to low-scoring bowlers, making the game more competitive against high-scoring bowlers.

LEAVE — The pins left standing after the first roll of a frame. *Example: 7-pin leave.*

OPEN FRAME — A frame in which neither a strike nor spare is rolled.

PERFECT GAME — Bowling 12 strikes in a row. The score of a perfect game is 300.

PIN COUNT — The number of pins knocked down on a given roll. Often called "pinfall" or "count".

PIN SCATTER — When pins are knocked down by other pins. Also called "pin action".

POCKET — The ideal place to hit the pins to increase the chance of rolling a strike.

RELEASE — When the ball leaves the bowler's hand after the approach.

SCRATCH SCORE — The basic game total.

SHADOW BOWLING — This is a practice or warm-up in which bowlers roll balls down a lane that has no pins. This is done to practice technique and ball motion.

SHUT-OUT — When a team rolls enough points to make it mathematically impossible for the opposing team to catch up and win or tie.

SLIDING FOOT — The bowler's foot that slides on the lane after the ball is rolled. If you are right-handed, you will have a left sliding foot. If you are left-handed, you will have a right sliding foot.

TIMING — The time in which the hand releases the ball and the sliding foot slides.

BOWLING ETIQUETTE

Some of you may be wondering — *What exactly does "etiquette" mean?*

Etiquette simply means polite behavior when you are around others. It's a big way of saying you need to follow the rules. **PLEASE** show other bowlers the proper respect and obey the rules of the game. It will make bowling a lot more fun. And remember, if you treat **OTHERS** with respect, they will treat **YOU** with respect! Here are some basic things you need to know.

BOWLING SHOES — Wear your bowling shoes **AT ALL TIMES** when you are on the bowling lane. Bowling shoes not only help you bowl better, they keep the bowling lane from being damaged. Neatly tuck your street shoes away so no one trips or falls over them. A good place for them is under your chair.

DON'T BE TOO LOUD — Bowling can be exciting and it's fun to cheer and shout. But do so only when it is appropriate. Excessive shouting and loud talking can be distracting to other bowlers. Do not use bad words or insult other bowlers.

NEVER GET IN THE WAY OF OTHER BOWLERS — This can interfere with their roll and it could lead to an injury. Whenever you are not bowling, try to stay seated or away from the lane. Stay off the approach when it is not your turn and do not take too long on the approach when it is your turn.

KEEP THE LANE AND YOUR AREA CLEAN — Don't throw candy wrappers, food or other items in or around the lane. Keep your area tidy and clean. Remember, other bowlers will be using your lane next. You wouldn't like to sit down in someone else's garbage, so don't make others sit in yours.

BE READY WHEN IT IS YOUR TURN — No one wants to try to find you when it is your turn to bowl. It slows down the game and upsets the other bowlers' rhythm.

WHO GOES FIRST? — If two bowlers are about to bowl at the same time, the bowler to the right should be allowed to go first.

STEP OFF THE APPROACH AFTER YOU HAVE BOWLED YOUR FRAME — Once you've completed your frame, it is time to step away from the approach and sit down.

WAIT FOR THE PINSETTER — If you roll your ball before the pinsetter is done and the sweeper bar is not clear, you may damage your ball *and* the machine!

BOWL IN YOUR OWN LANE — If you accidentally bowl in the wrong lane, this will delay the game and the score will have to be corrected. If you see someone about to bowl in the wrong lane, make sure to politely tell him or her.

USE YOUR OWN BALL — Make sure to keep track of which ball is yours. If you have to use another player's ball, ask for permission first.

HAVE FUN — Every bowler wants to win every game. If you don't win or if you just have an off day, remember that you'll have more opportunities to improve your game. Be happy for the person or team who bowls well and congratulate them.

AFTER THE GAME — Clean up your area and take all your personal belongings with you. Remove your bowling ball from the ball return and bring back any balls that belong to the alley. Remove and return your rented shoes.

HOW TO KEEP SCORE

A game of bowling is made up of 10 frames. In each frame, the bowler is given two chances to knock over the ten pins at the end of the bowling lane. If the bowler knocks down all ten pins on the first or second roll in the tenth and final frame the bowler earns a bonus roll. Below is an example of a completed ten-frame game for one bowler who scored a total of **140**.

1	2	3	4	5	6	7	8	9	10
6 2	7 /	5 4	X	X	7 2	6 3	5 –	8 /	9 / X
8	23	32	59	78	87	96	101	120	140

We will take you step-by-step to show you exactly how we arrived at this total. Remember, keeping score in bowling is not always easy and can take time to learn. Follow along as we to see how one bowler's game is scored. Although modern bowling alleys use automatic scorers, it's good to understand how you got your score. OK — Let's get started!

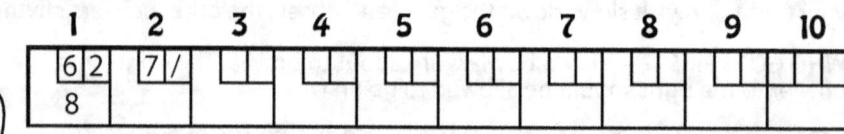

FRAME ONE: The bowler knocks down six pins on the first roll. Place a **6** in the first box in frame number one. The bowler rolls again. On the second roll, the bowler knocks down two pins. Place a **2** in next box. The numbers are totaled **6 + 2 = 8** and the score is entered as **8**. Because the bowler has left pins standing, the bowler now sits down and awaits his or her next turn.

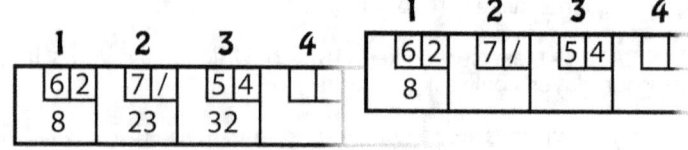

FRAME TWO: The bowler knocks down seven pins on the first roll. Place a **7** in the first box in frame number two. The bowler rolls again. On the second roll, the bowler knocks down the remaining three pins for a *SPARE*. Place a diagonal line " **/** " next to the **7** to indicate a *SPARE*. The numbers are totaled **7 + 3 = 10** but are **NOT** entered into the frame at this point. Why? Because whenever a *SPARE* (or *STRIKE*) is rolled, the bowler gets a *BONUS ROLL* and moves on to the next frame. *Frames are only totaled when a bowler fails to knock down all ten pins.*

1	2	3	4		1	2	3	4
6 2	7 /	5 4			6 2	7 /	5 4	
8	23	32			8			

FRAME THREE: The bowler knocks down five pins on the first roll. Place a **5** in the first box in frame number three. The bowler rolls again. On the second roll, the bowler knocks down four pins. Place a **4** in the next box. Because the bowler did **NOT** roll a *STRIKE* or a *SPARE*, his or her turn is over. Now total frame two: Take the **8** from frame one and add it to the total of frame two and add **ONLY** the first roll from frame three: **8 + (7 + 3) + 5 = 23**.

Next, total frame three. Take the **23** from frame two and add it to the total of frame three: **23 + (5 + 4) = 32**. Because the bowler **DID NOT** roll a *STRIKE* or a *SPARE* and has left pins standing, the bowler now sits down and waits for his or her next turn.

	1	2	3	4	5	6	7	8	9	10
4	6 2	7 /	5 4	X						
	8	23	32							

FRAME FOUR: The bowler knocks down all ten pins. This is called a *STRIKE*. Place an "**X**" in the first box. A strike is worth ten points, **BUT IT IS NOT ENTERED YET!** Remember, a *STRIKE* is similar to a *SPARE*. Whenever a *STRIKE* is rolled, the bowler gets a *BONUS ROLL* and moves on to the next frame.

> **NOTE:** For team and league bowling, everyone bowls one frame as a team, then moves on to the next frame. **EXAMPLE:** With a five-person team, the first bowler bowls frames 1 and 6, the second bowler bowls frames 2 and 7 and so on.

	1	2	3	4	5	6	7	8	9	10
5	6 2	7 /	5 4	X	X					
	8	23	32							

FRAME FIVE: The bowler again knocks down all ten pins. This is called a *DOUBLE*. Place an "**X**" in the first box. **DO NOT** enter the ten points yet. The bowler gets a *BONUS ROLL* and moves on to the next frame.

	1	2	3	4	5	6	7	8	9	10
6	6 2	7 /	5 4	X	X	7 2				
	8	23	32							

FRAME SIX: The bowler knocks down seven pins on the first roll. Place a **7** in the first box. The bowler rolls again. On the second roll, the bowler knocks down two pins. Place a **2** in the next box. Because the bowler did *NOT* roll a *STRIKE* or a *SPARE*, his or her turn is over. Now total frames four, five, and six as follows:

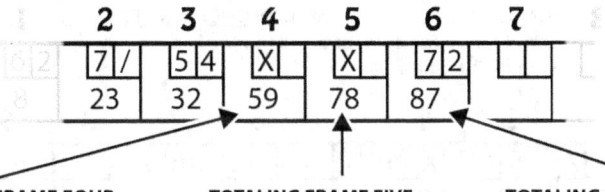

TOTALING FRAME FOUR	**TOTALING FRAME FIVE**	**TOTALING FRAME SIX**
Take **32** from frame three and add it to both *STRIKES* and the first roll from frame six.	Take **59** from frame four and add it to the *STRIKE* from frame five and the **total** from frame six.	Take the **78** from frame five and add it to the total from frame six.
32 + 10 + 10 + 7 = 59	59 + 10 + (7 + 2) = 78	78 + (7 + 2) = 87
		Because the bowler did **NOT** roll a *STRIKE* or a *SPARE*, the bowler's turn is over.
NOTE: Because two *STRIKES* were bowled in a row, only the first roll from frame six is included in the total for frame four.	**NOTE:** Because this is the last *STRIKE* bowled, **both** rolls from frame six are included in the total for frame five.	

	1	2	3	4	5	6	7	8	9	10
7	6 2	7 /	5 4	X	X	7 2	6 3			
	8	23	32	59	78	87	96			

FRAME SEVEN: The bowler knocks down six pins on the first roll. Place a **6** in the first box in frame number seven. The bowler rolls again. On the second roll, the bowler knocks down three pins. Place a **3** in the next box. Because the bowler did **NOT** roll a *STRIKE* or a *SPARE*, the bowler's turn is over. Now total frame seven. Take the **87** from frame six and add it to the total from frame seven: 87 + (6 + 3) = **96**.

	1	2	3	4	5	6	7	8	9	10
8	6 | 2	7 | /	5 | 4	X	X	7 | 2	6 | 3	5 | –		
	8	23	32	59	78	87	96	101		

FRAME EIGHT: The bowler knocks down five pins on the first roll. Place a **5** in the first box. The bowler rolls again. On the second roll, the bowler misses all the pins. Place a horizontal dash "—" in the next box to represent the *MISS* which equals <u>ZERO</u>. Because the bowler did <u>NOT</u> roll a *STRIKE* or a *SPARE*, the bowler's turn is over. Now total frame eight. Take the **96** from frame seven and add it to the total from frame eight: 96 + 5 = 101.

	1	2	3	4	5	6	7	8	9	10
9	6 | 2	7 | /	5 | 4	X	X	7 | 2	6 | 3	5 | –	8 | /	
	8	23	32	59	78	87	96	101		

FRAME NINE: The bowler knocks down eight pins on the first roll. Place an **8** in the first box. The bowler rolls again. On the second roll, the bowler knocks down the remaining two pins for a *SPARE*. Place a diagonal line " **/** " next to the **8** to indicate a *SPARE*, giving this frame a total of **10**. And remember, whenever a *SPARE* (or *STRIKE*) is rolled, the bowler's turn continues in to the next frame. <u>FRAME NINE WILL NOT BE TOTALED UNTIL FRAME TEN IS COMPLETED.</u>

	1	2	3	4	5	6	7	8	9	10
10	6 | 2	7 | /	5 | 4	X	X	7 | 2	6 | 3	5 | –	8 | /	9 | / | X
	8	23	32	59	78	87	96	101		

FRAME TEN: The bowler knocks down nine pins on the first roll. Place a **9** in the first box. The bowler rolls again. On the second roll, the bowler knocks down the remaining one pin for a *SPARE*. Place a diagonal line " **/** " next to the **9** to indicate a *SPARE*. Because the bowler knocked down all ten pins, a **BONUS ROLL** is earned. <u>THIS CAN ONLY HAPPEN IN THE TENTH FRAME.</u> The bowler rolls the bonus ball for a *STRIKE*. Place an " **X** " in the last box. The game is now over and it's time to total the remaining frames.

1	2	3	4	5	6	7	8	9	10
6 | 2	7 | /	5 | 4	X	X	7 | 2	6 | 3	5 | –	8 | /	9 | / | X
8	23	32	59	78	87	96	101	120	140

TOTALING FRAME NINE
Take **101** from frame eight and add it to the *SPARE and* the first roll from frame ten.
101 + (8 + 2) + 9 = 120

TOTALING FRAME TEN
Take **120** from frame nine and add it to the *SPARE* and the bonus **10**.
120 + (9 +1) + 10 = 140

NOTE: All the points are totaled in the tenth frame, even if they are *STRIKES*.

THIS BOWLER SCORED A TOTAL OF 140

SCORING GUIDE

1st BOX → ← 2nd BOX
FRAME →

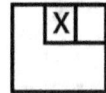

X STRIKE Scoring result of **10** points for a frame in which all ten pins are knocked down on the first roll. For the frame, the bowler scores **10** points PLUS *BONUS* points for <u>all the pins</u> knocked down in the next frame.

    DOUBLE Two strikes in a row.
        Scoring for the first frame of the double:
          First frame + second frame + first roll in the third frame.
        Scoring for the second frame of the double:
          Second frame + both rolls in the third frame.

    TURKEY Three strikes in a row.
        Scoring for the first frame of the turkey:
          Thirty points.
        Scoring for the second frame of the turkey:
          Second frame + third frame + first roll in the fourth frame.
        Scoring for the third frame of the turkey:
          Third frame + both rolls in the fourth frame.

    FOUR BAGGER Four strikes in a row.
    More than four:
    Five bagger,
    Six bagger,
    Seven bagger,
    etc...
        Scoring for the first and second frames of the four bagger:
          Thirty points for each frame.
        Scoring for the third frame of the four bagger:
          Third frame + fourth frame + first roll in the fifth frame.
        Scoring for the fourth frame of the four bagger:
          Fourth frame + both rolls in the fifth frame.

/ SPARE Scoring result of **10** points when the last of the ten pins are knocked down on the second roll of the frame. The bowler also scores *BONUS* points for the number of pins knocked down in <u>the first roll only</u> in the next frame.

— MISS Scoring result of **zero** points when a bowler knocks down no pins. Also called an *OPEN* frame, it is indicated with a horizontal dash "**—**" and can be entered in either box. If a ball goes into the gutters and bounces out and hits the pins, it will not count for any points.

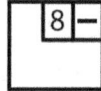

F FOUL This is when the bowler's swing arm goes over the foul line or the bowler's foot touches or slides over the foul line (foot foul). This is indicated with an "**F**". The bowler receives zero points and an "**F**" is placed in the appropriate box.

O SPLIT A spare in which the head pin is knocked down but at least two non-adjacent pins remain standing with a gap between them. Placing a circle around a number shows that the remaining pins are in the formation of a *SPLIT*. Instead of a circle, an "**S**" can be placed in front of the number to indicate the *SPLIT*.

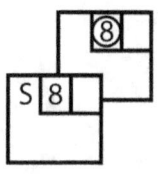

THE PERFECT GAME

A perfect game is the highest score possible. It is achieved by scoring a strike in every frame. This means that for every ball rolled, the bowler has knocked down *every pin on the first roll* of every frame, plus strikes on all three rolls in the tenth frame. That's **12** strikes in a row!

THE PERFECT STRIKE

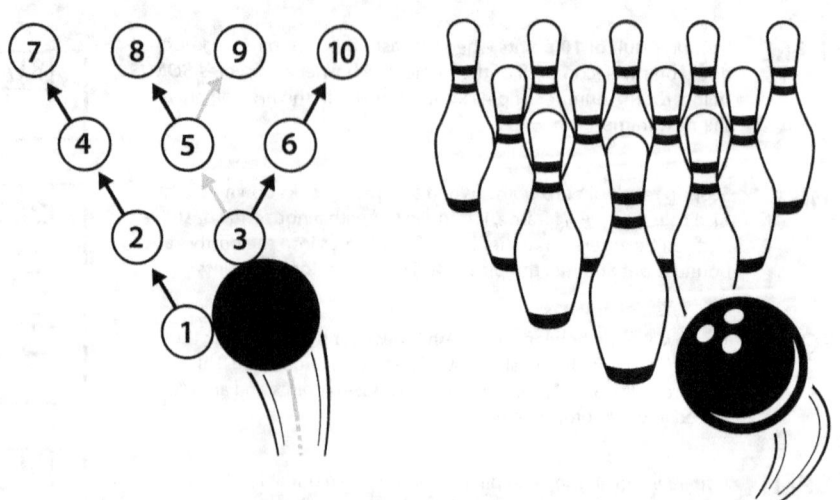

A perfect strike is when the ball hits only the **1, 3, 5** and **9** pins (if you are right-handed) or the **1, 2, 5** and **8** (if you are left-handed). The remaining pins are knocked over by other pins. This is known as *pin scatter* or *pin action*.

ALLEY GATOR™

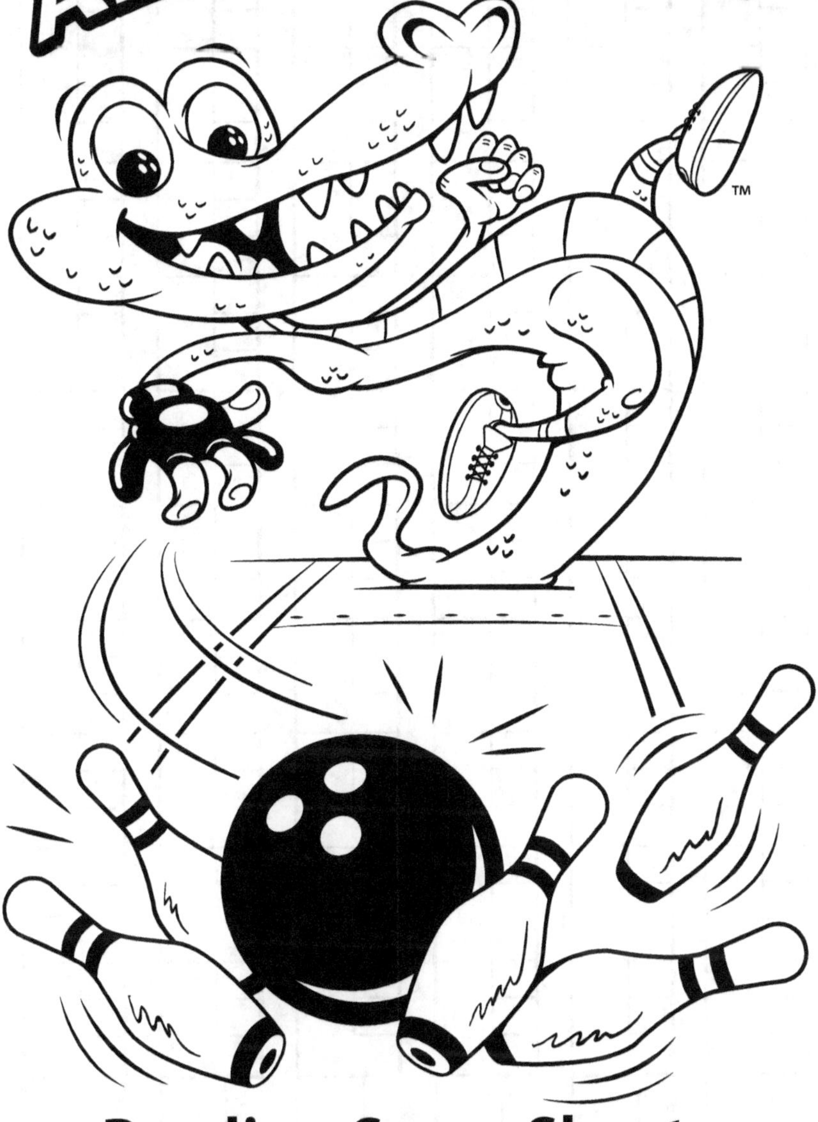

Bowling Score Sheets

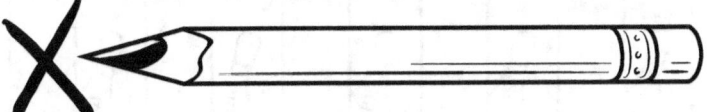

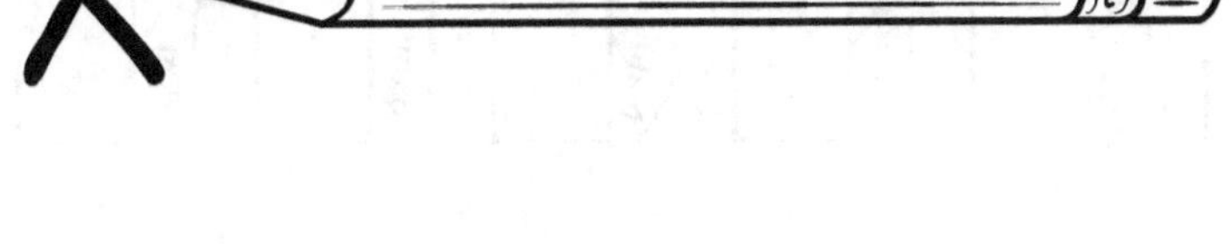

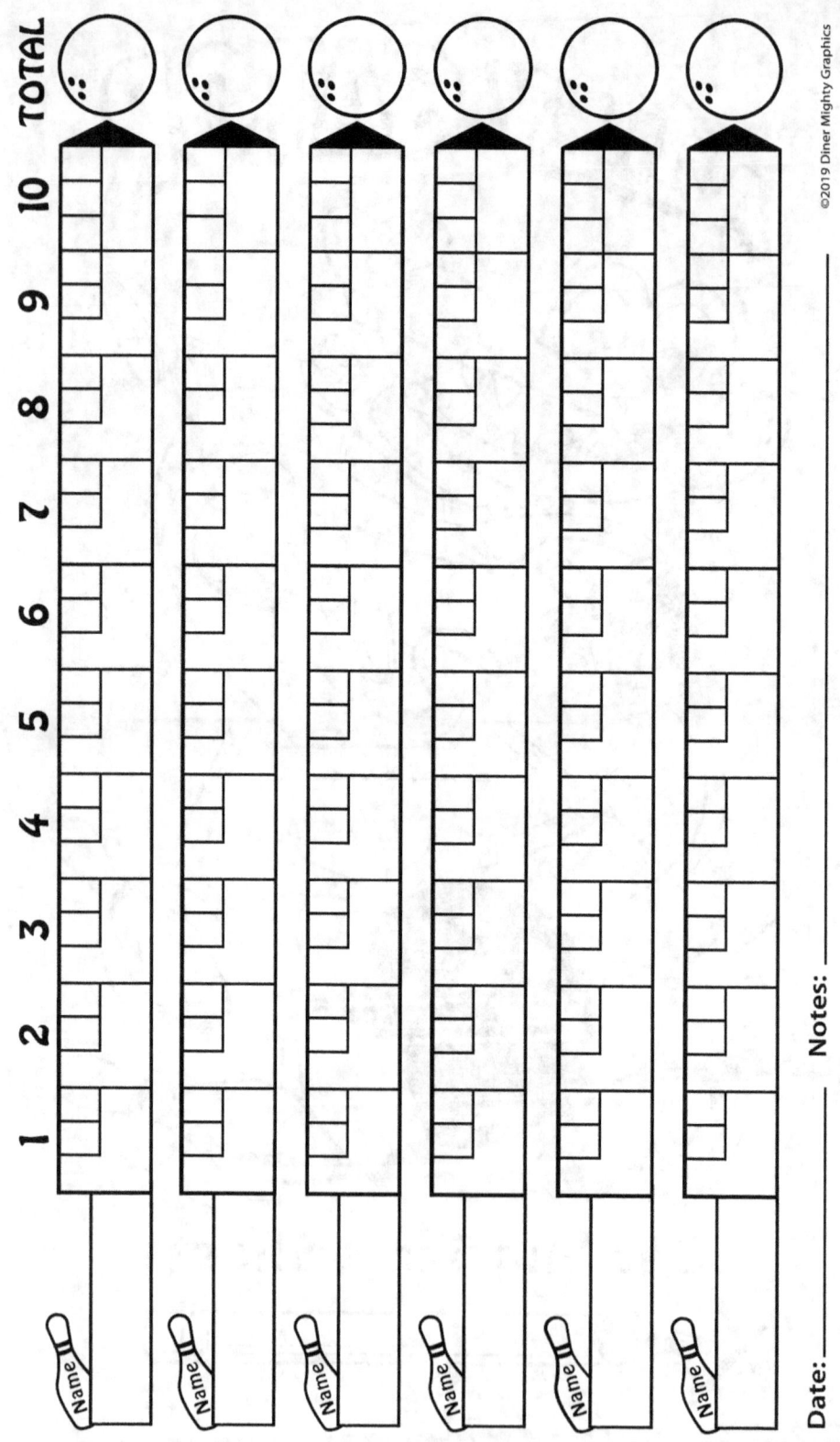

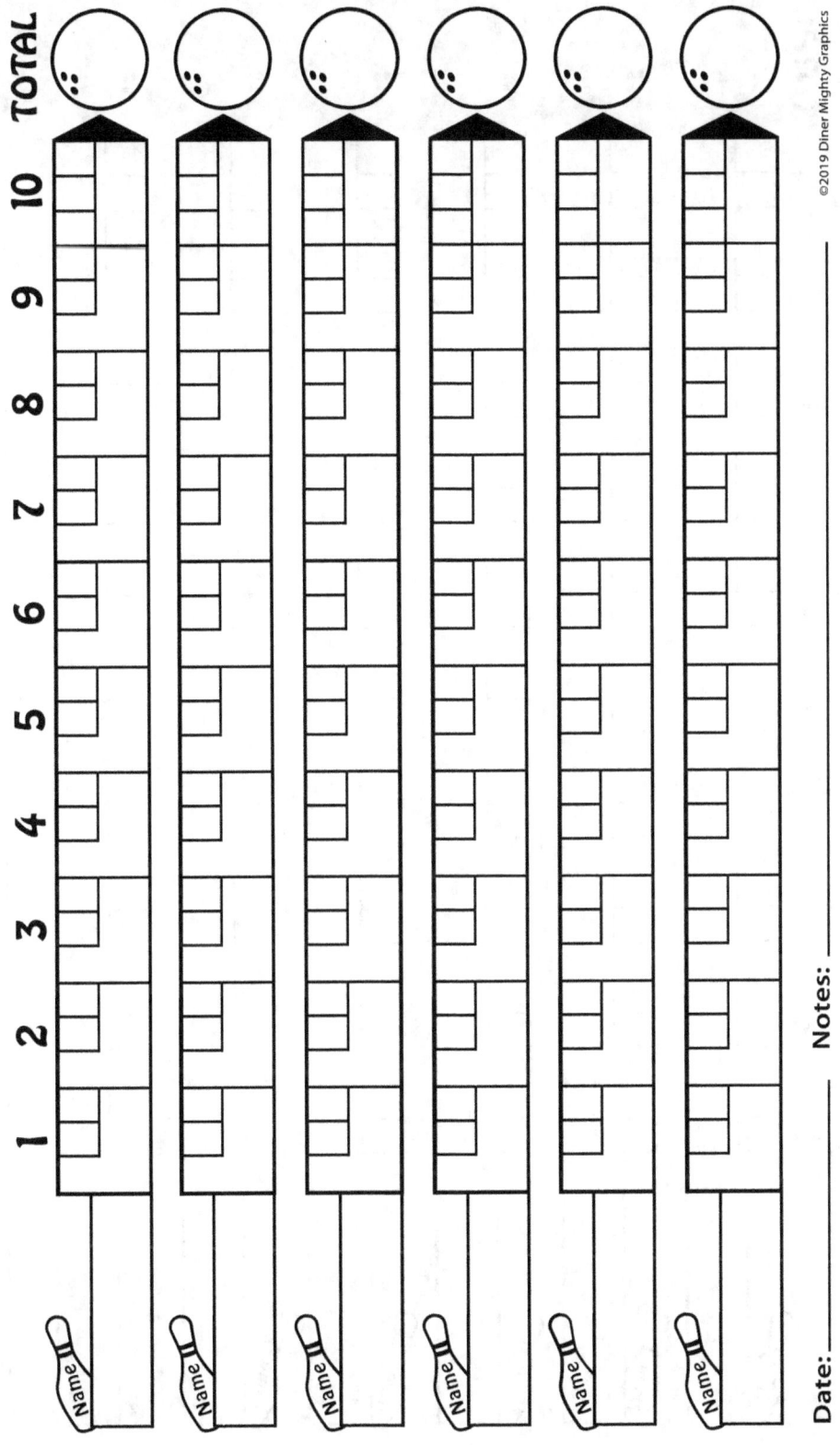

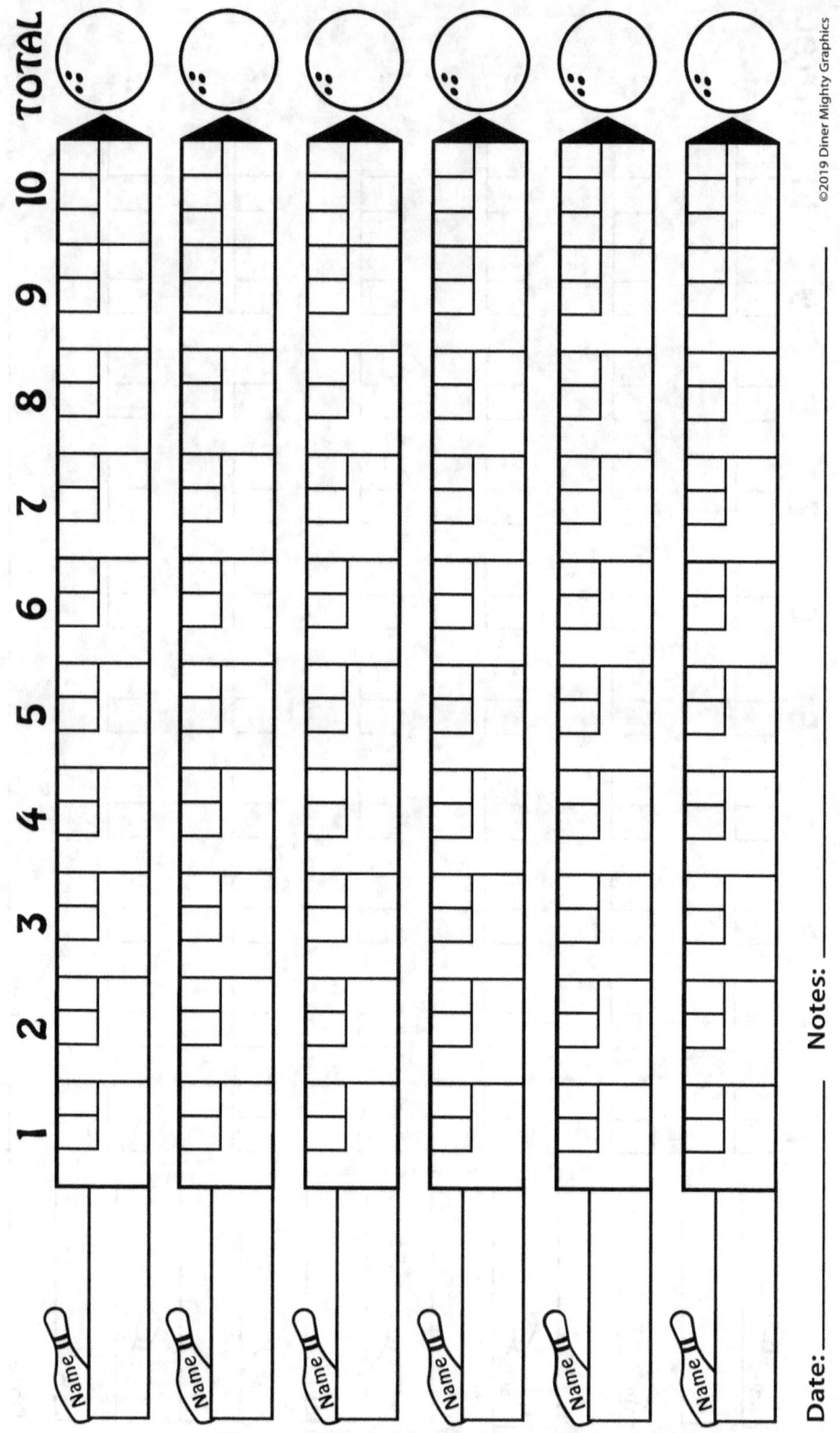

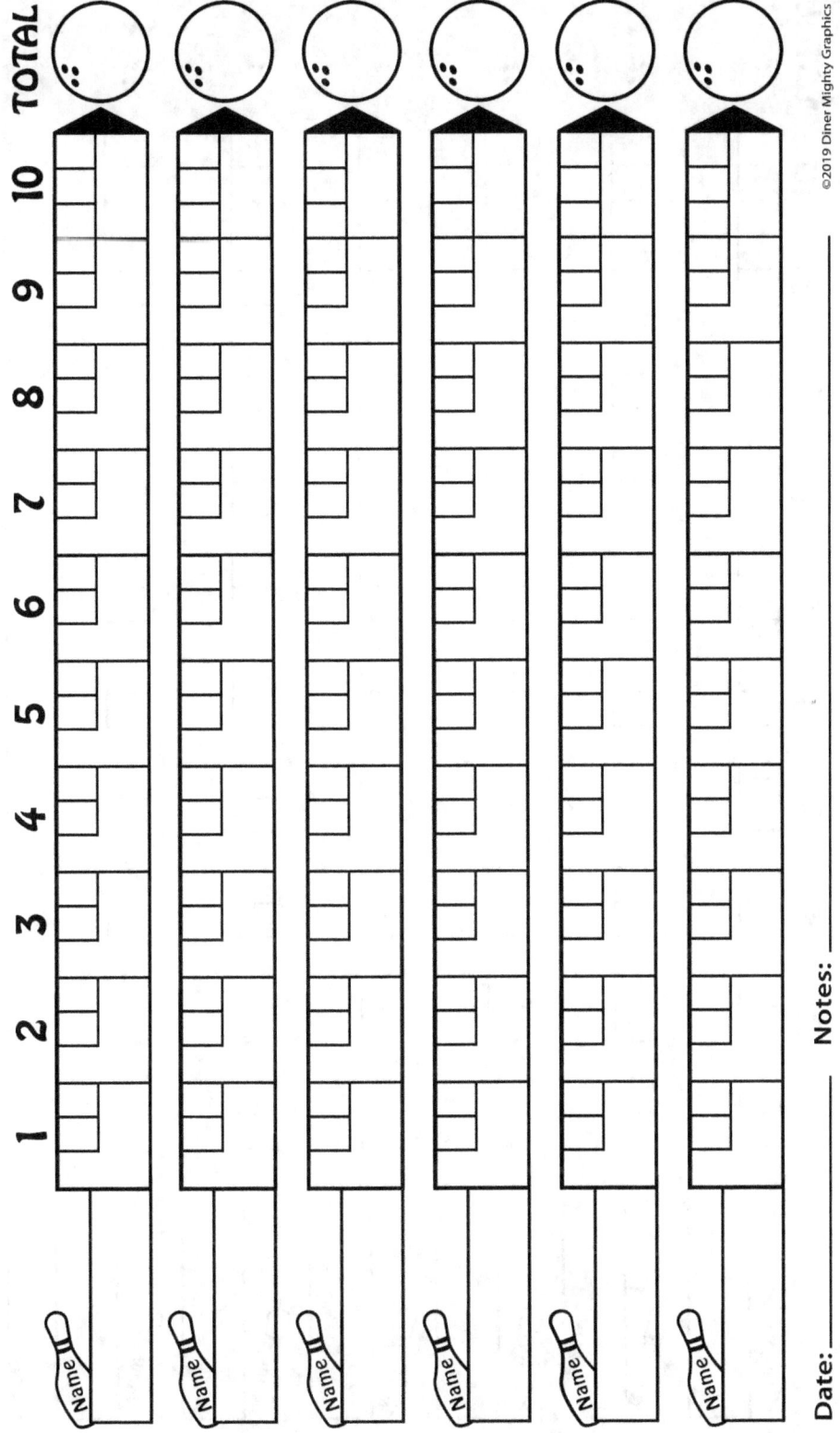

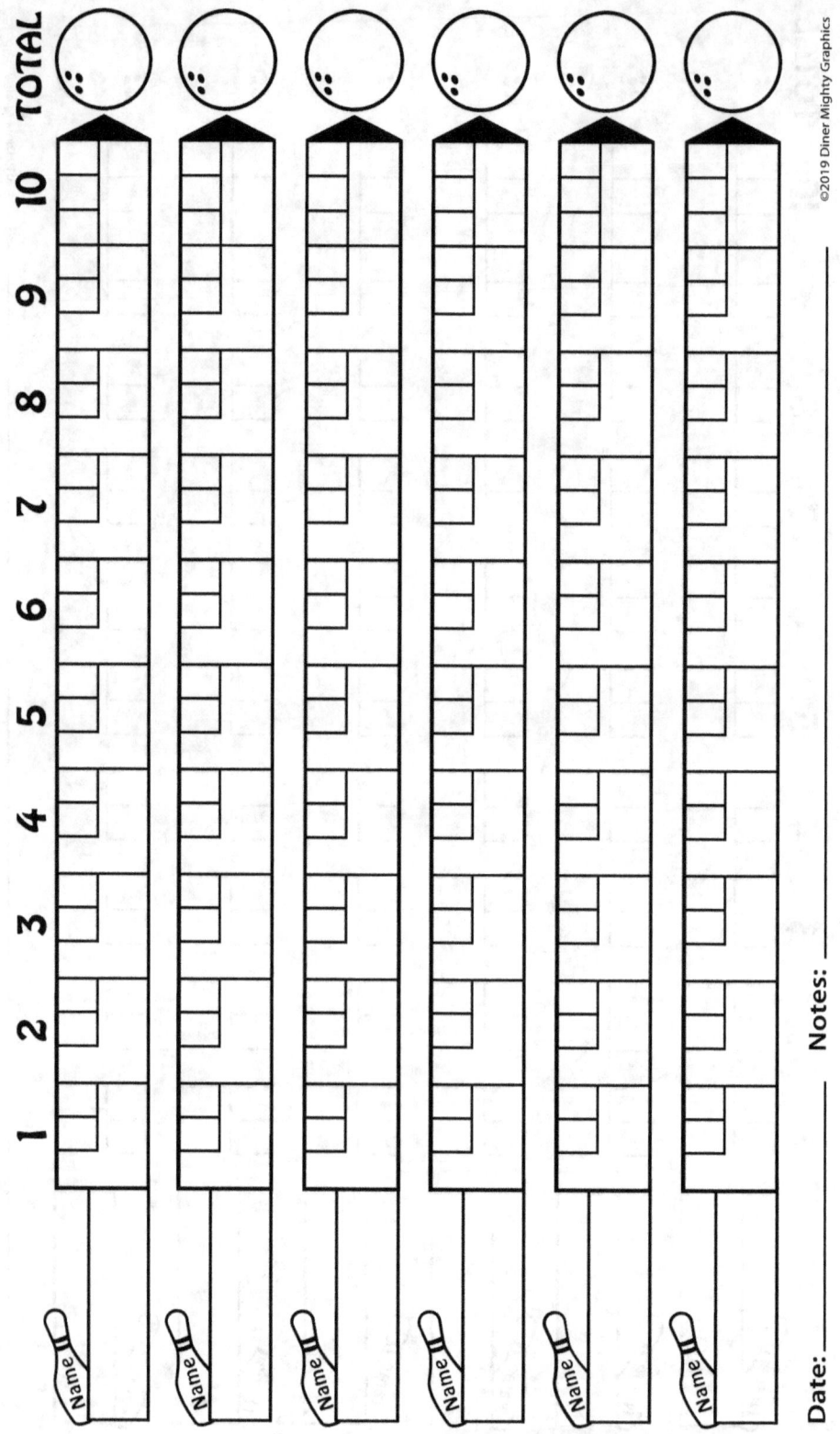

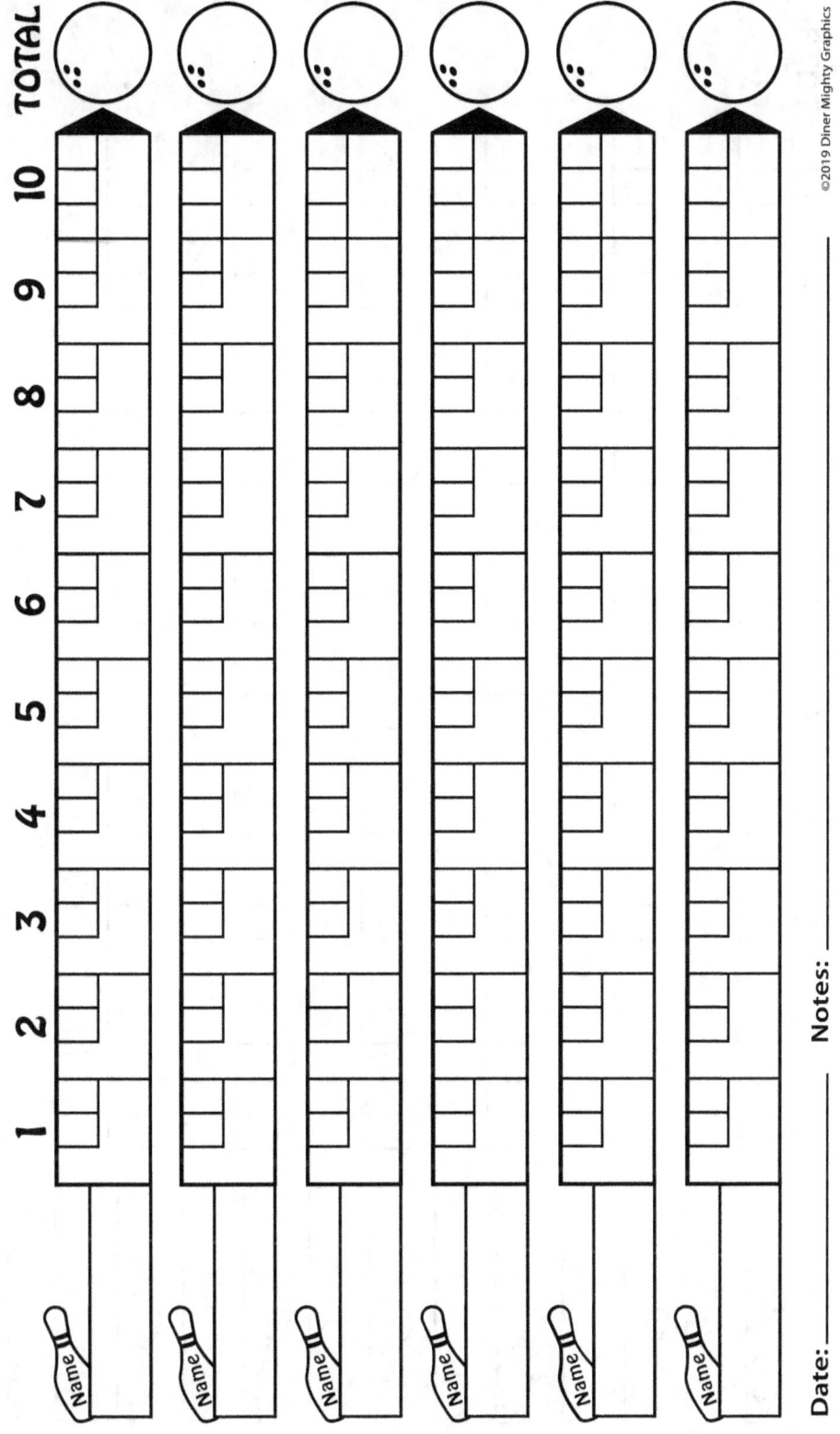

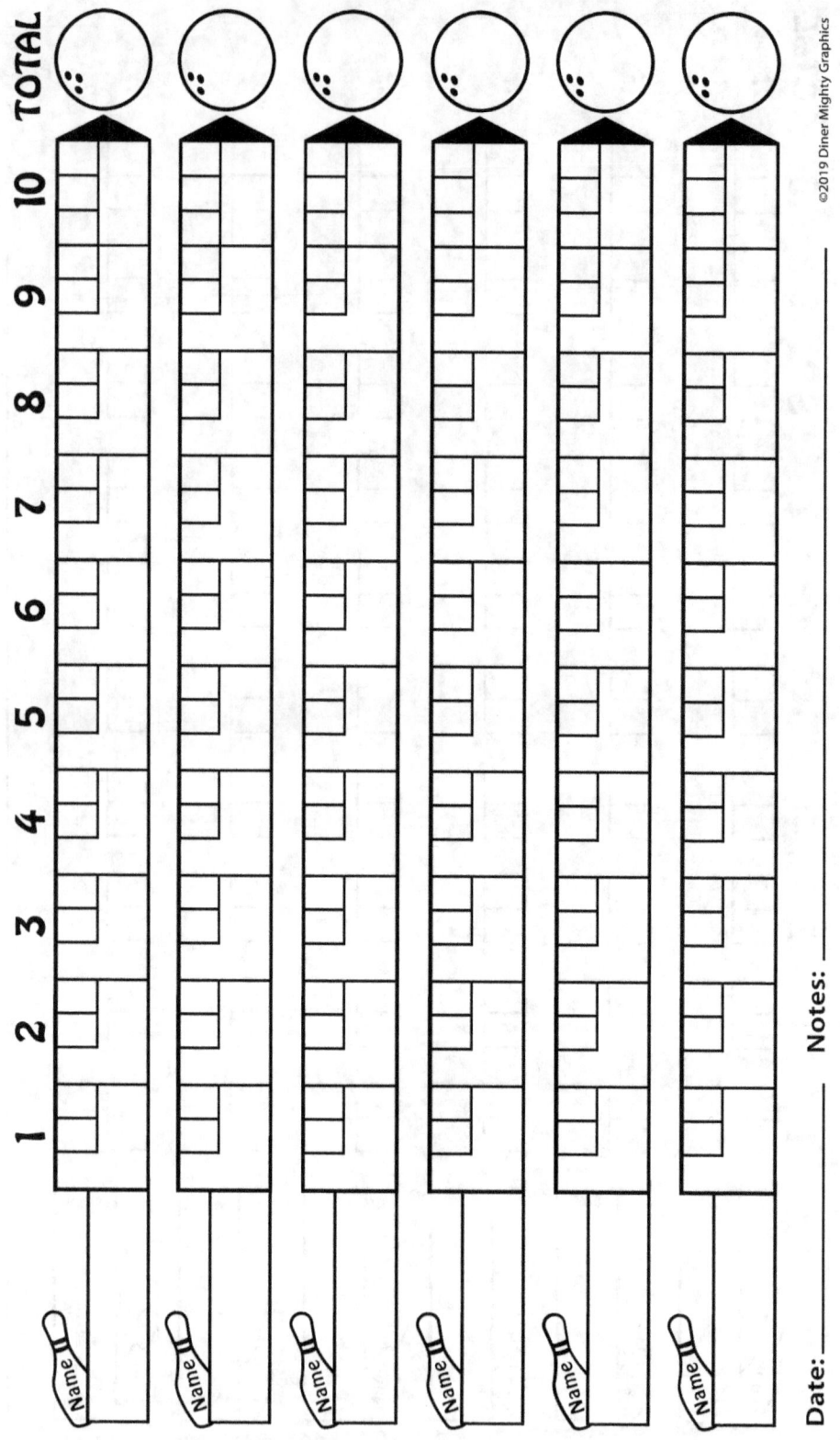

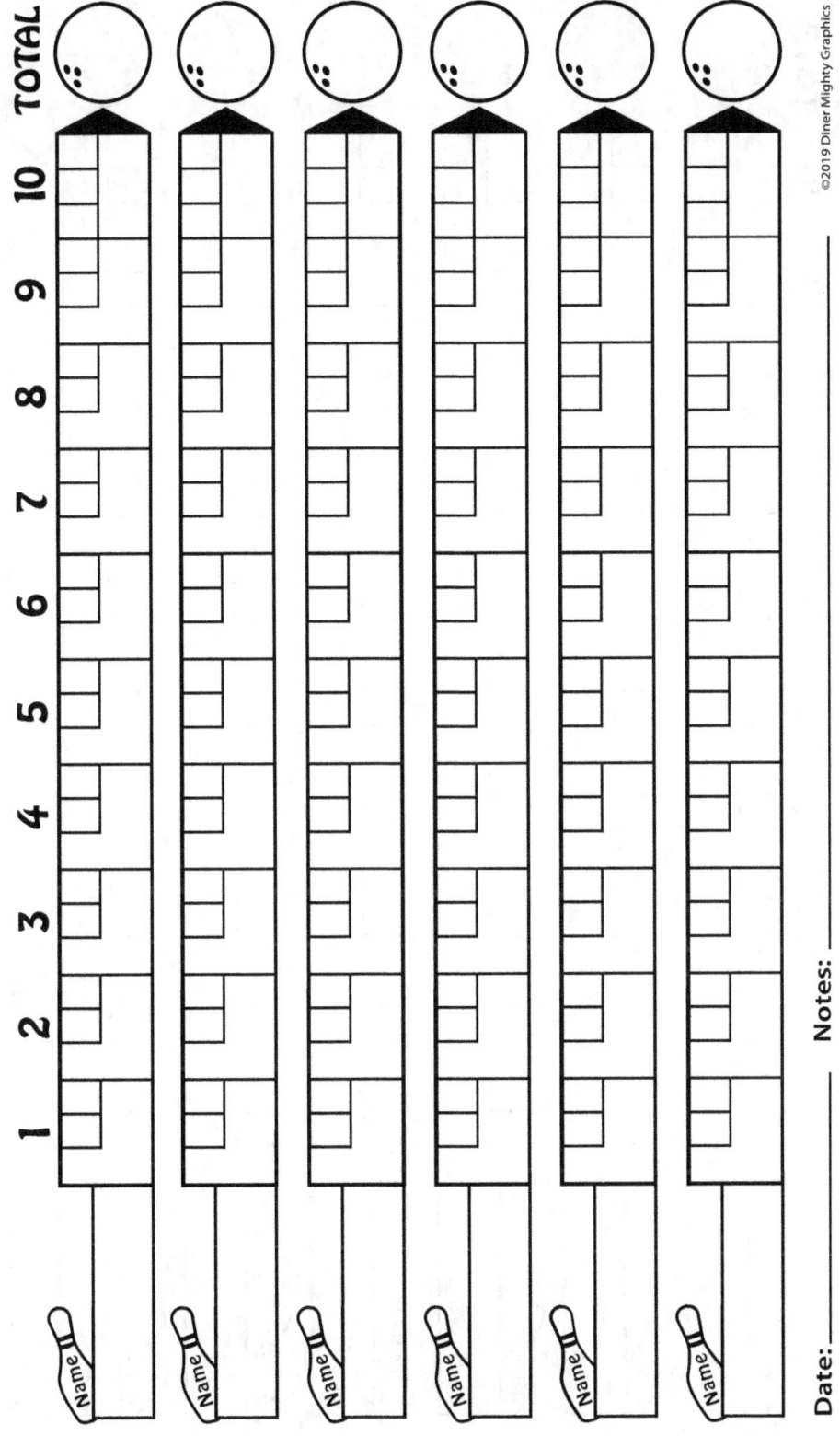

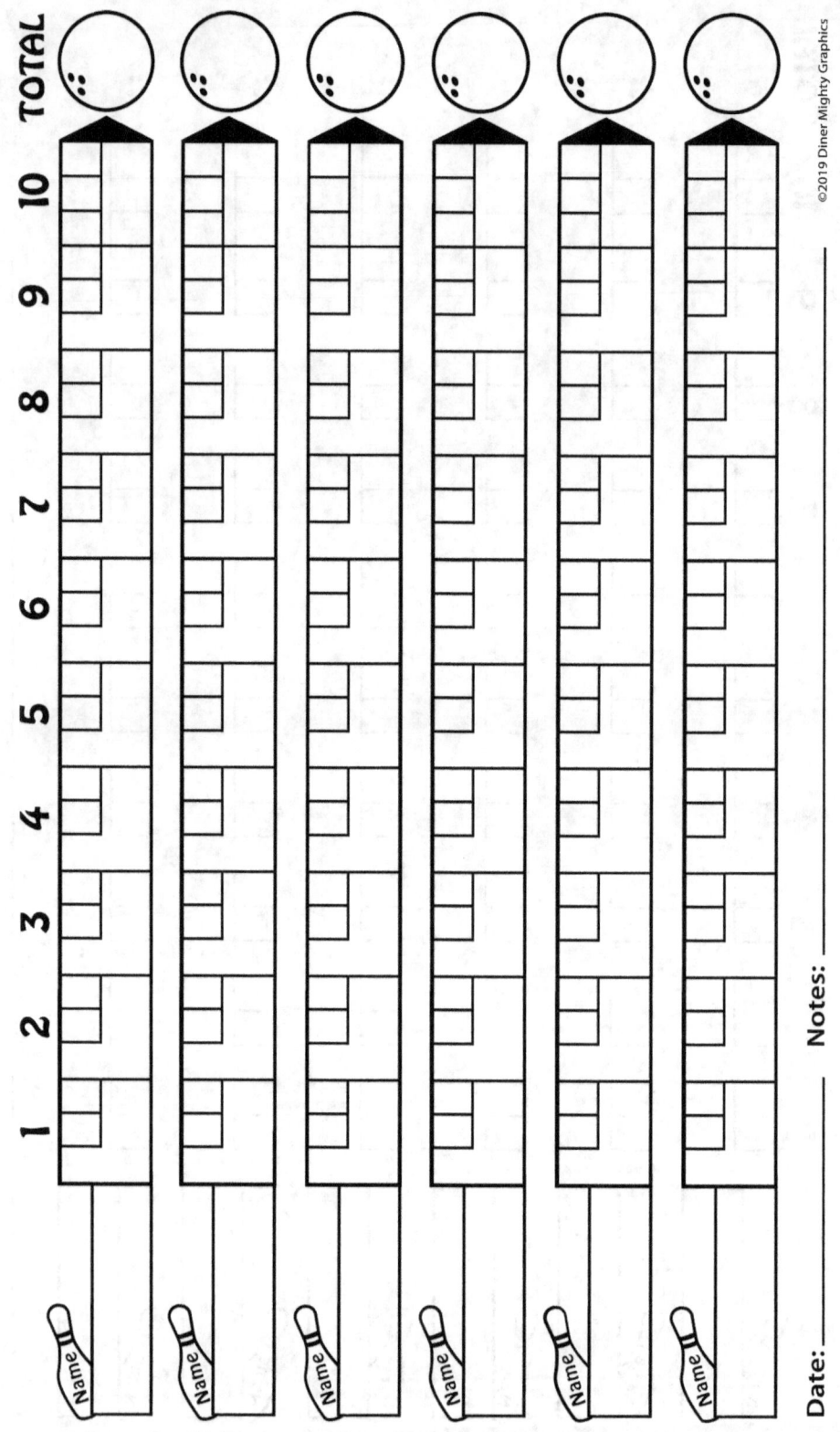

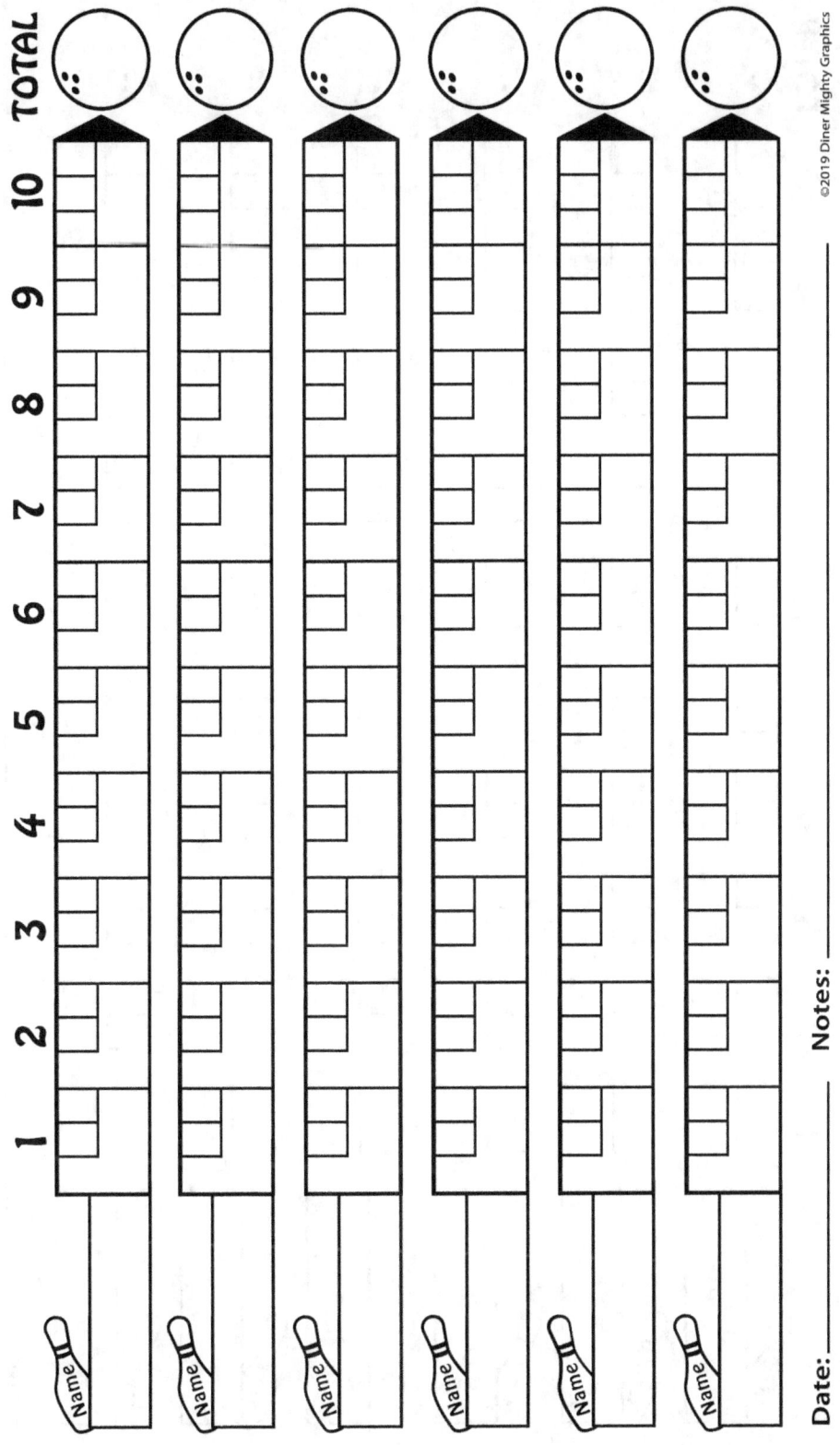

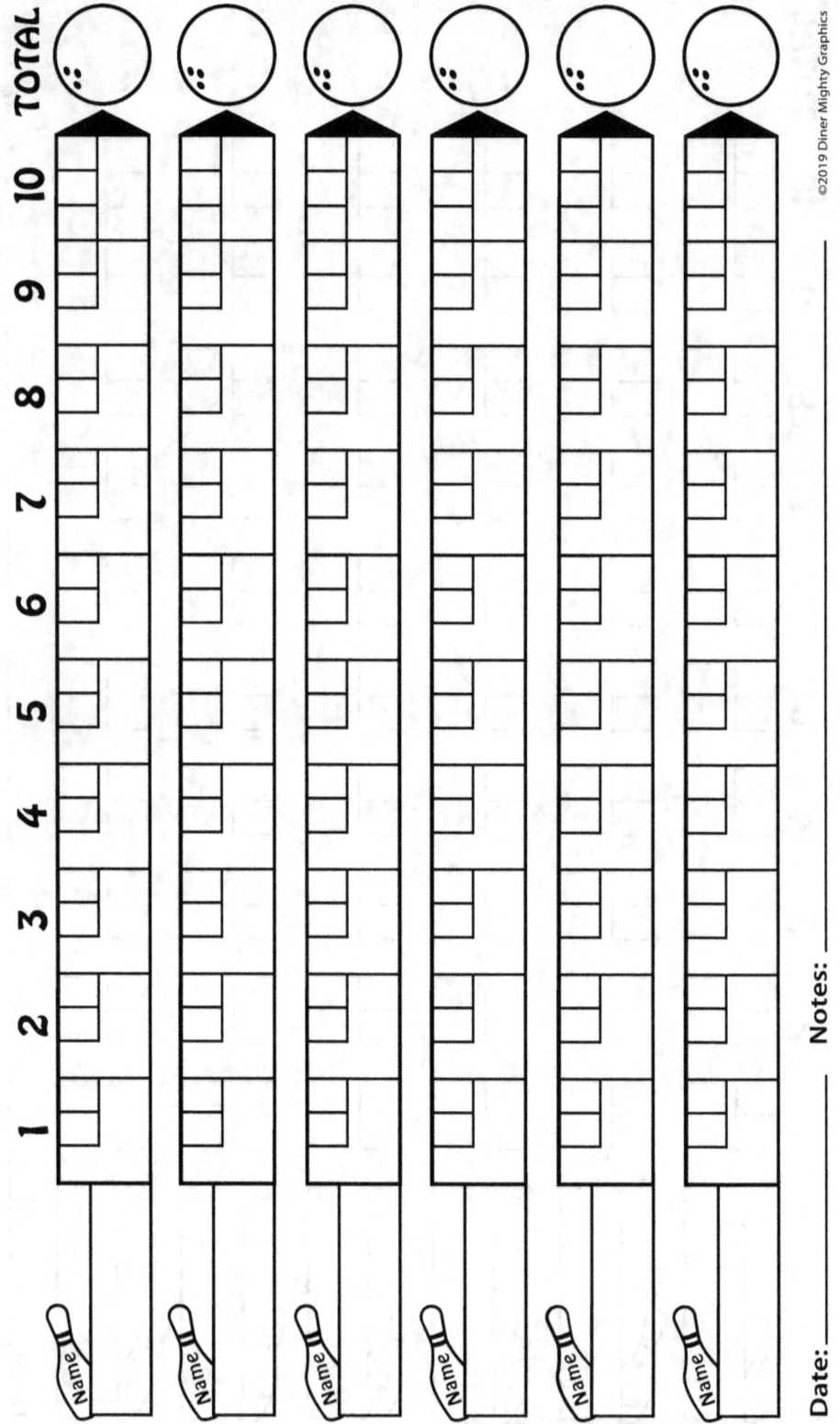

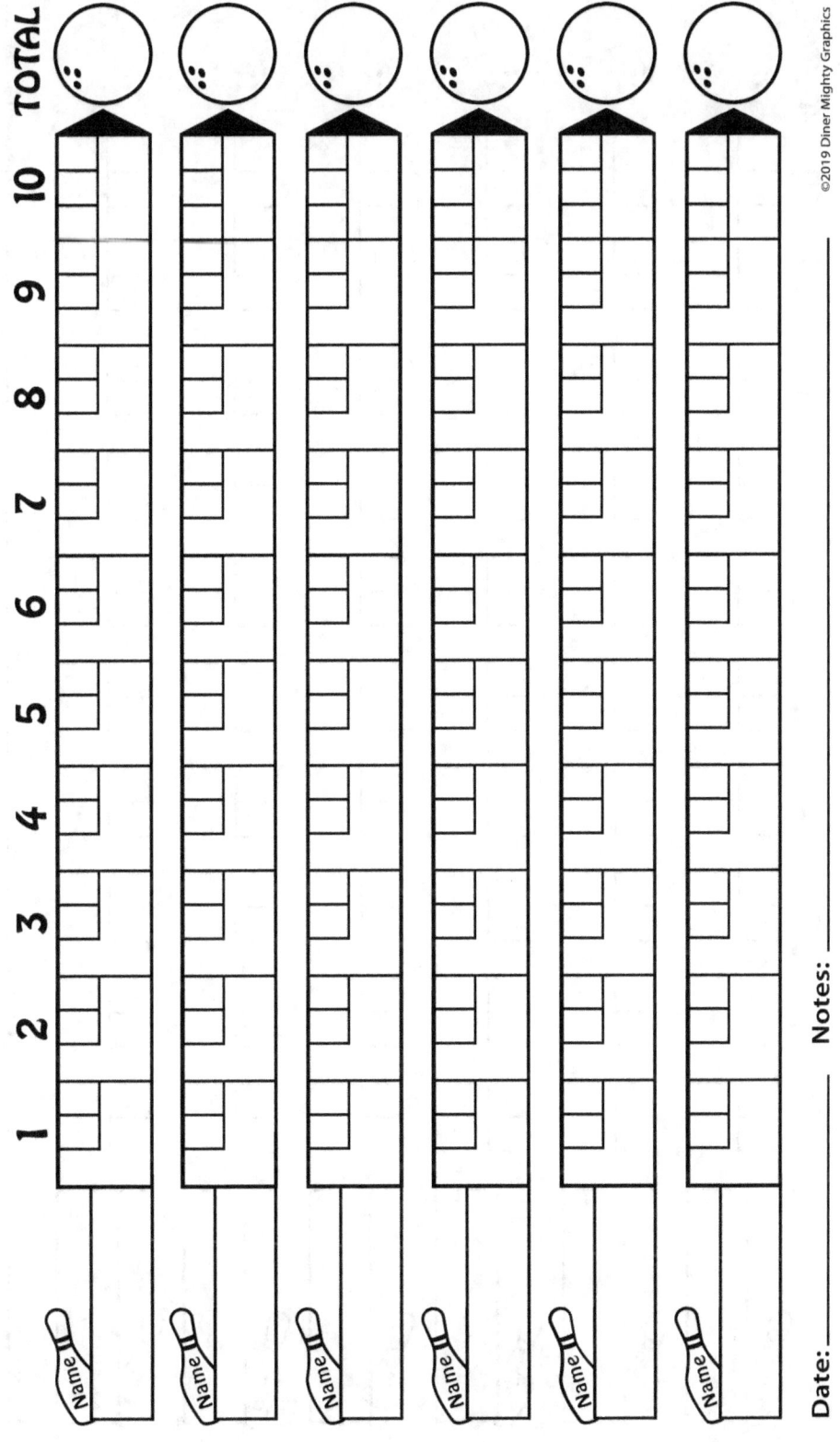

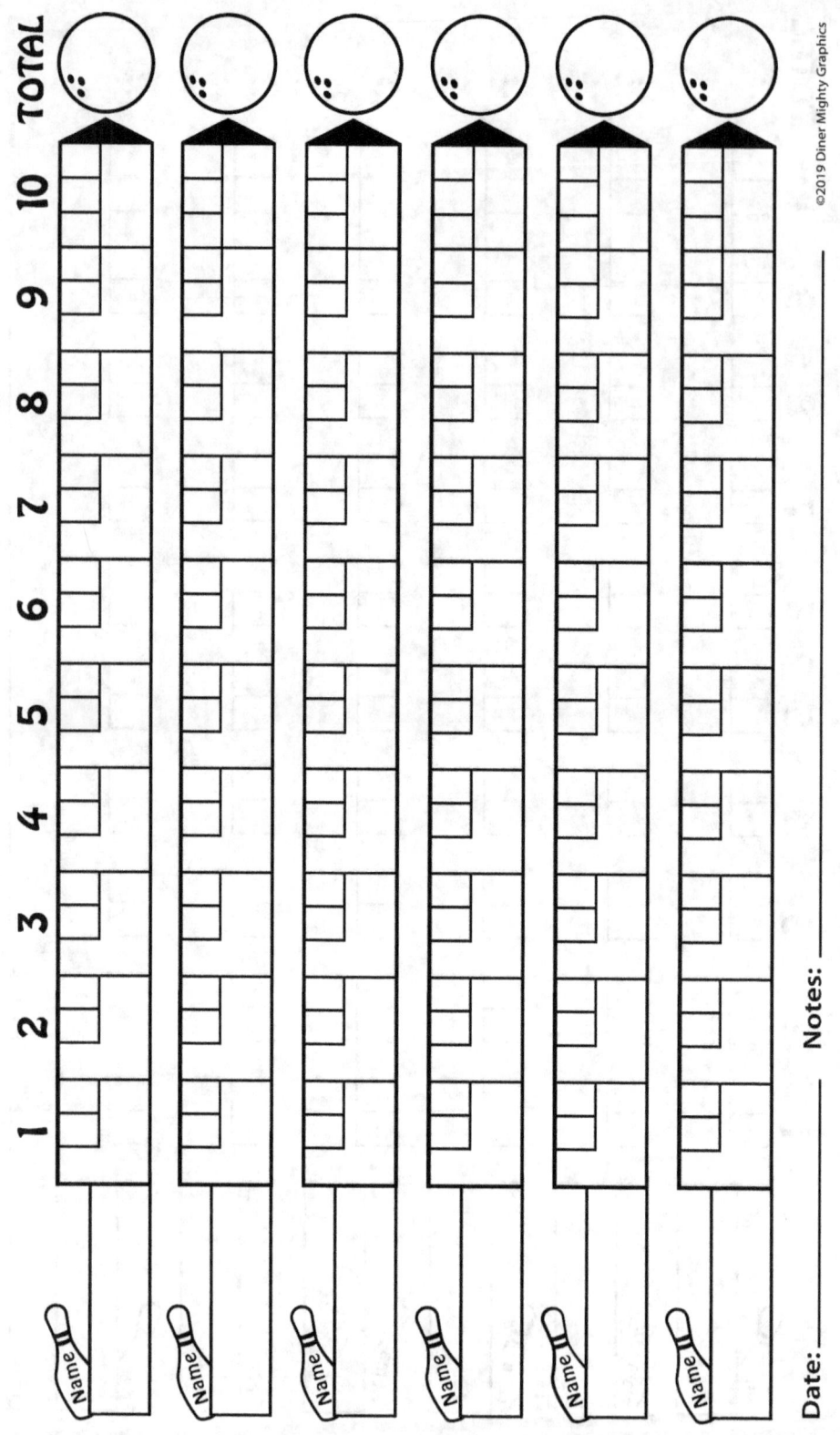

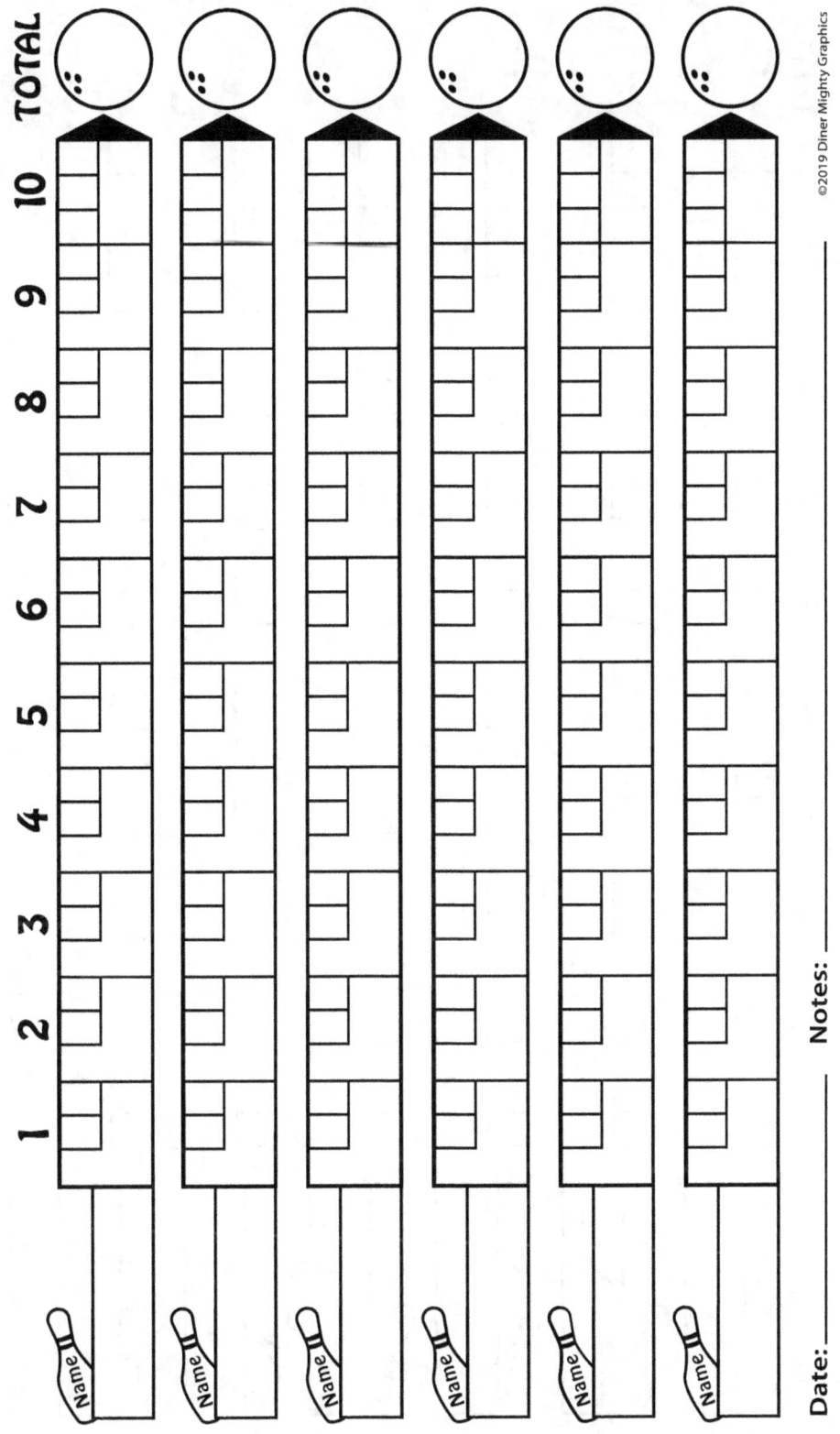

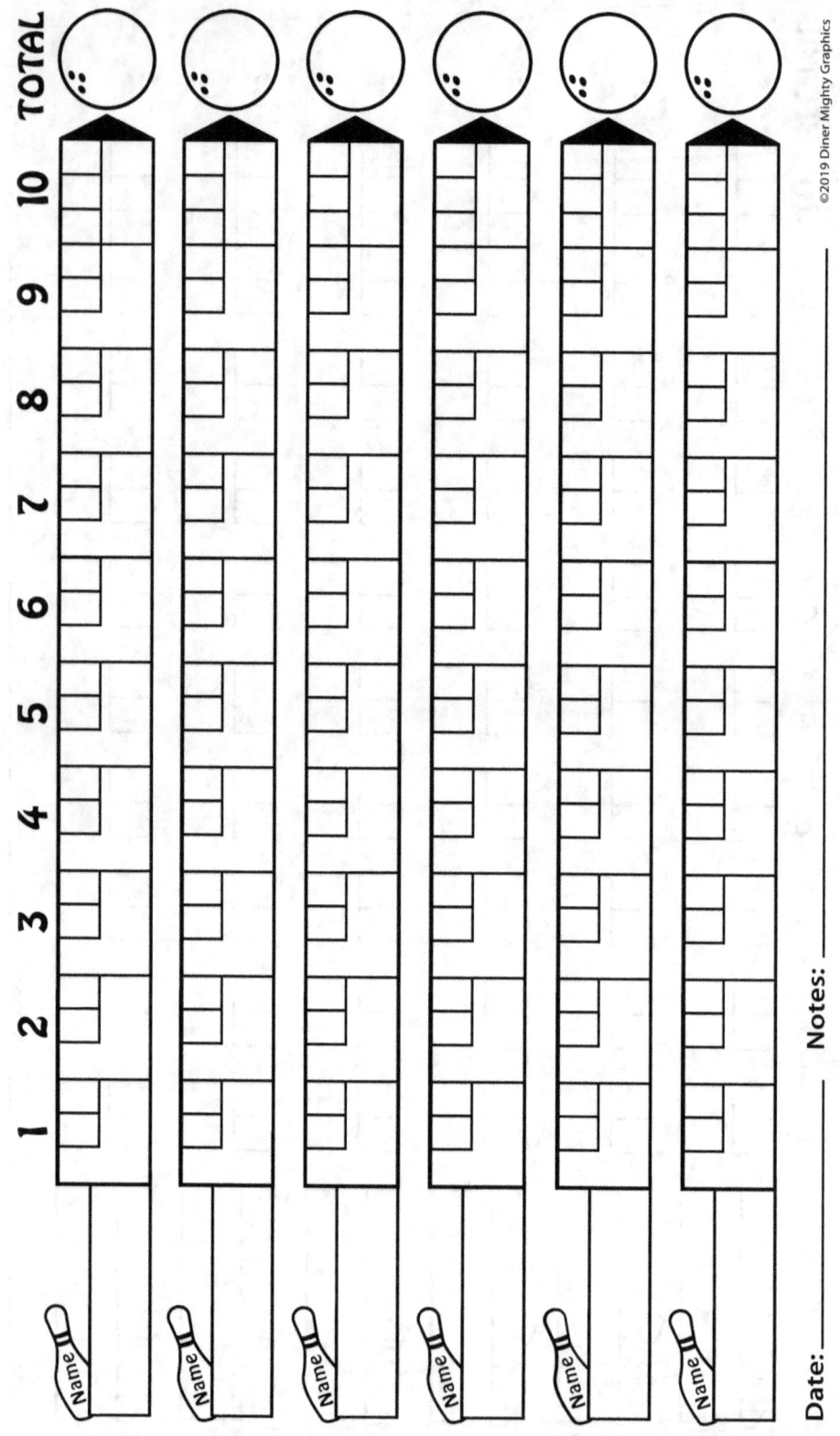

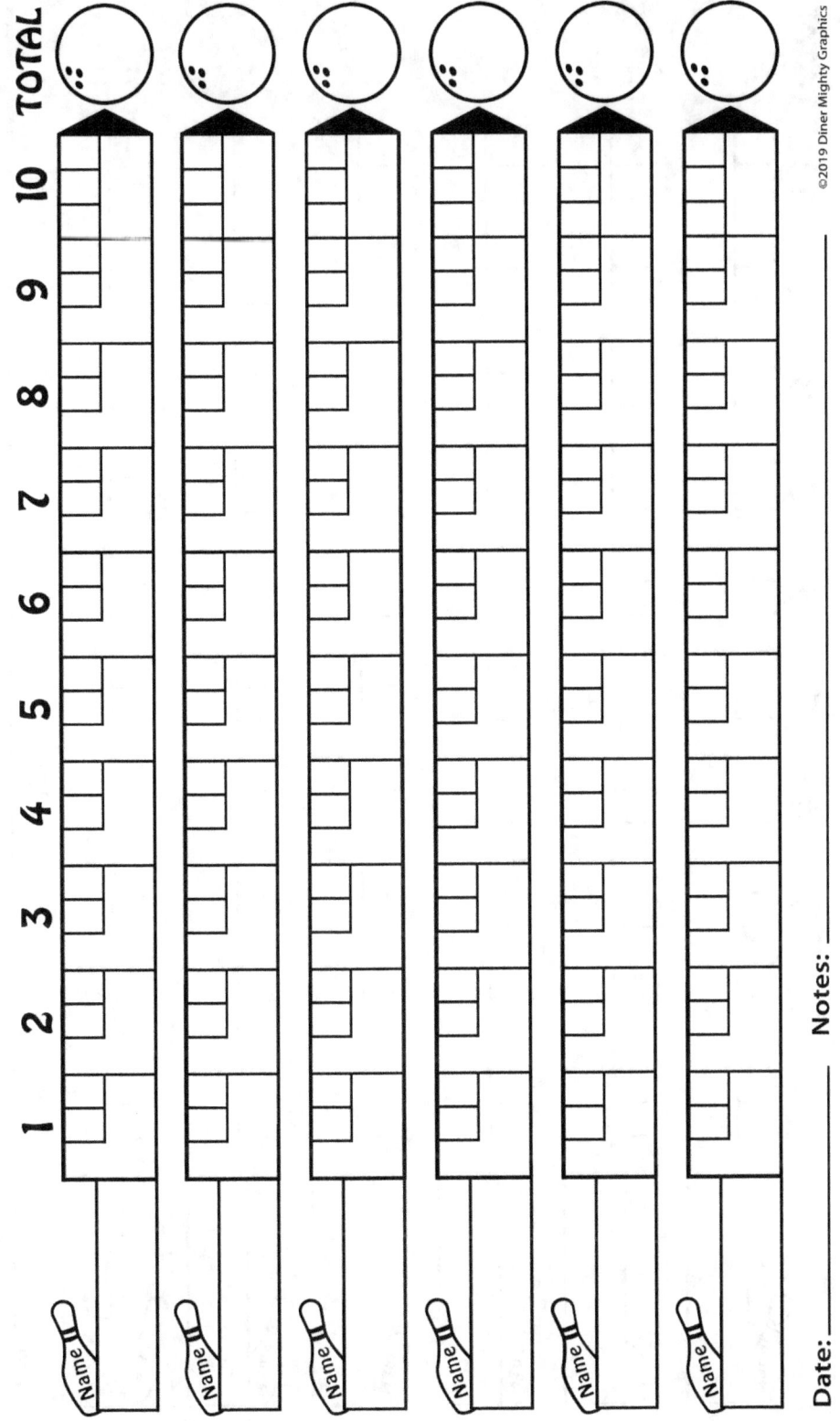

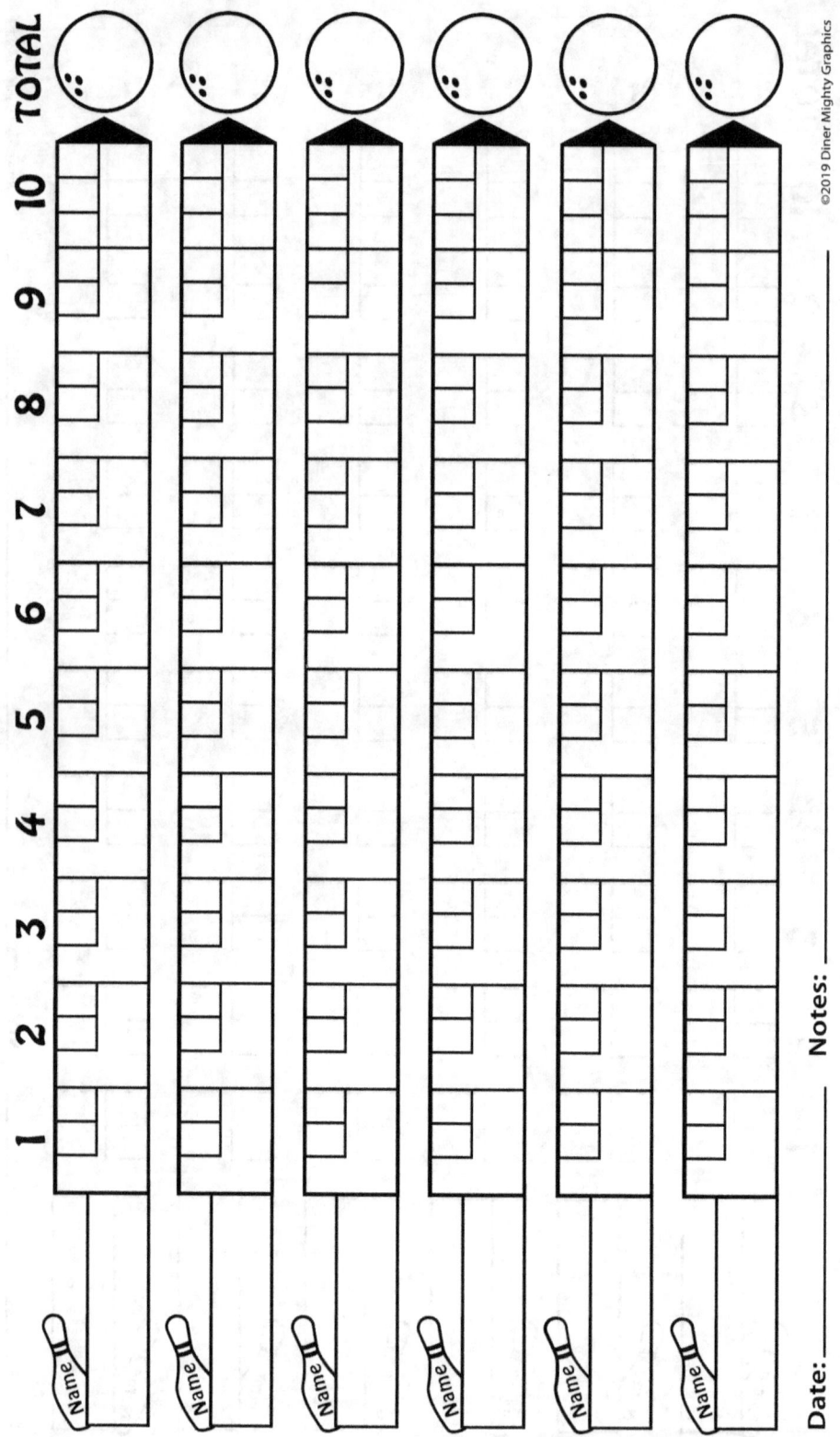

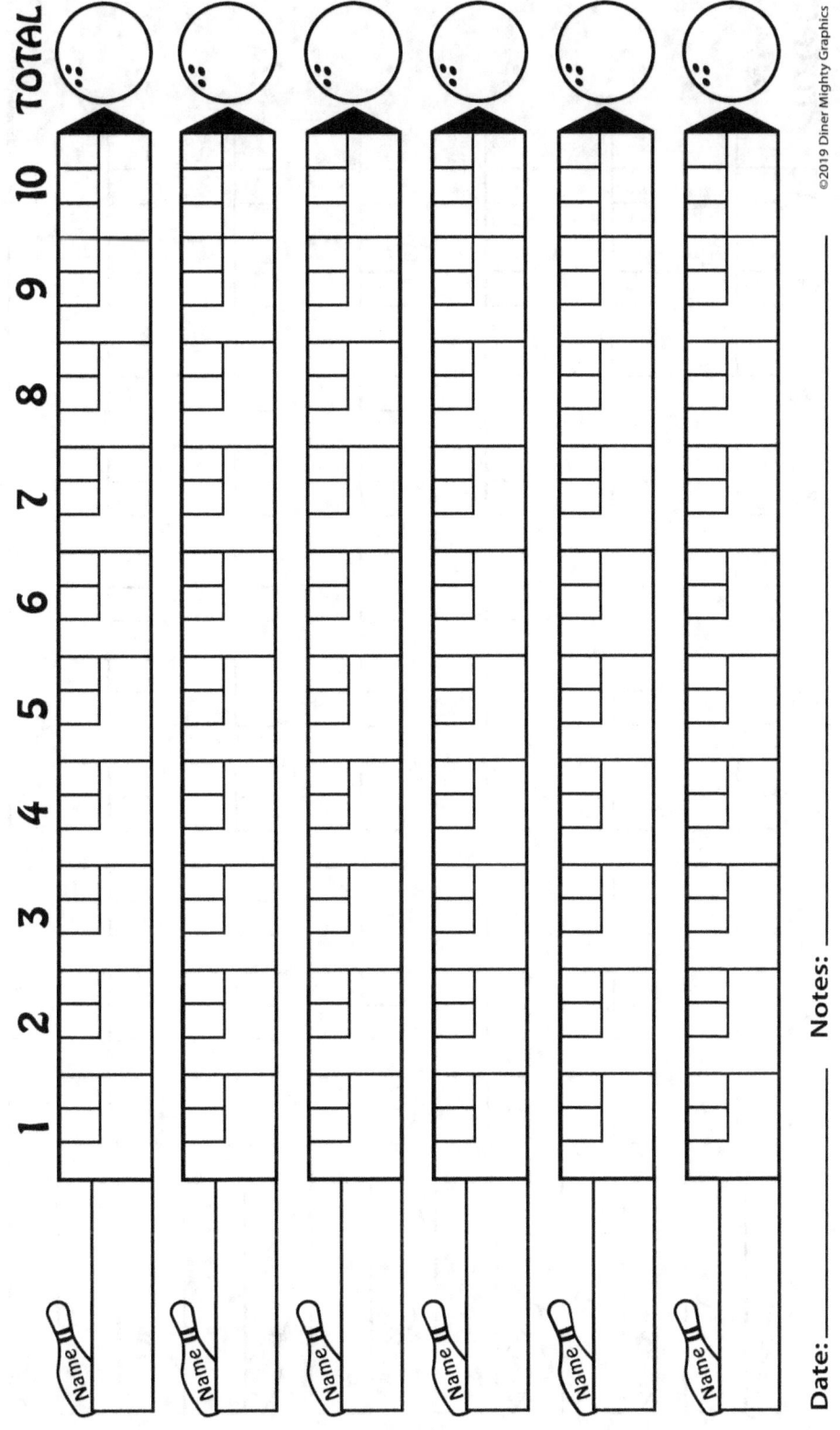

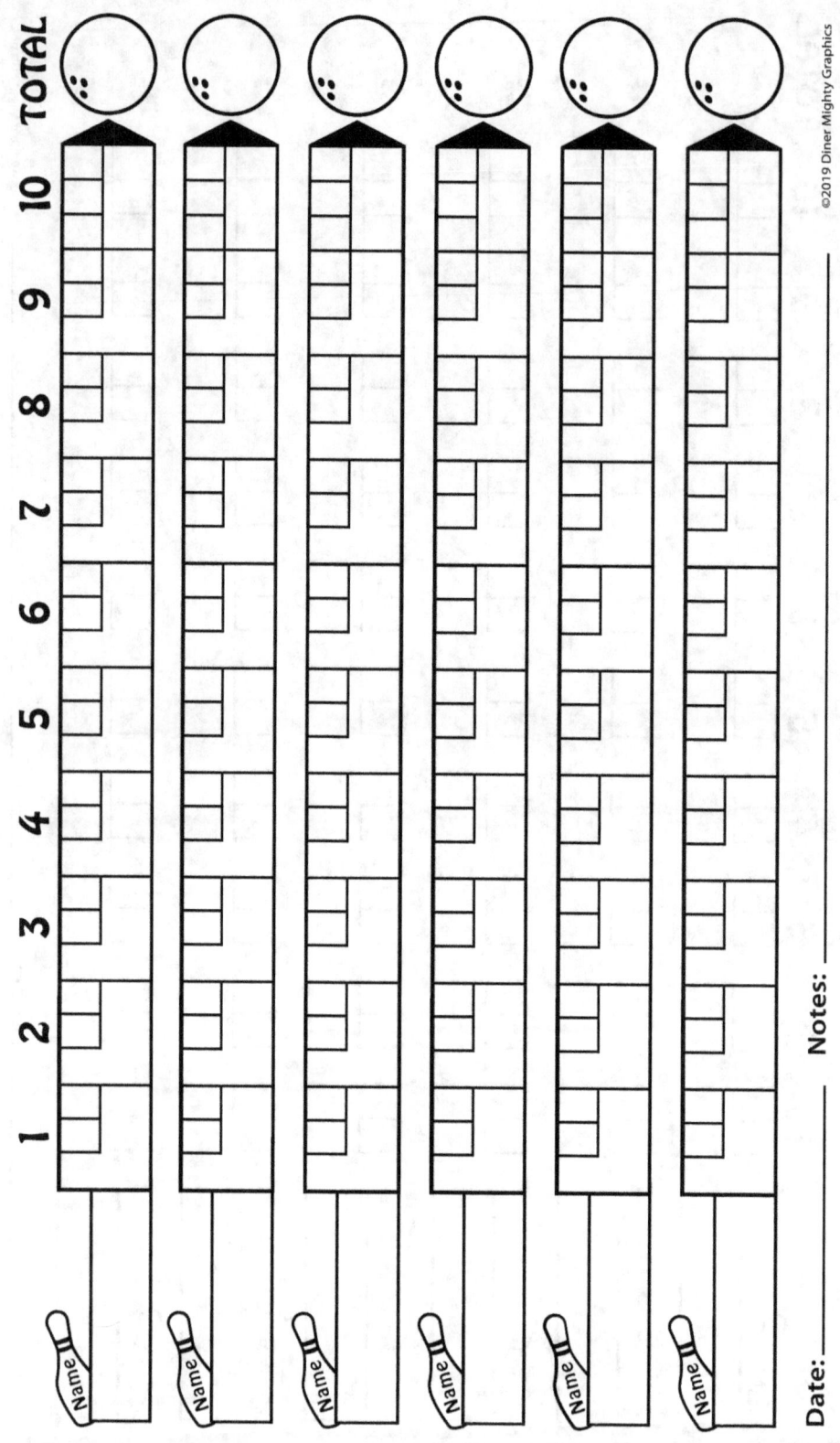

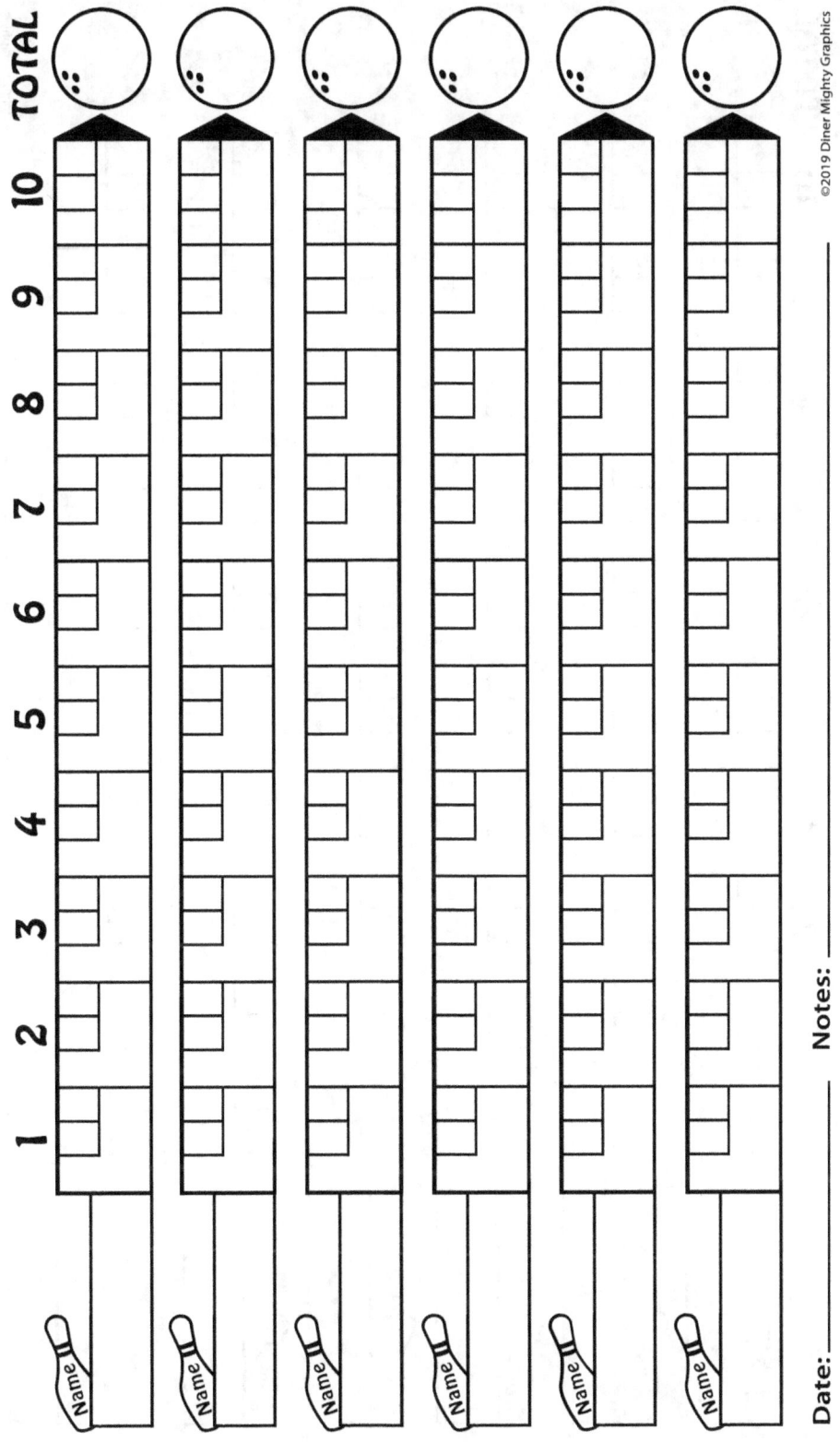

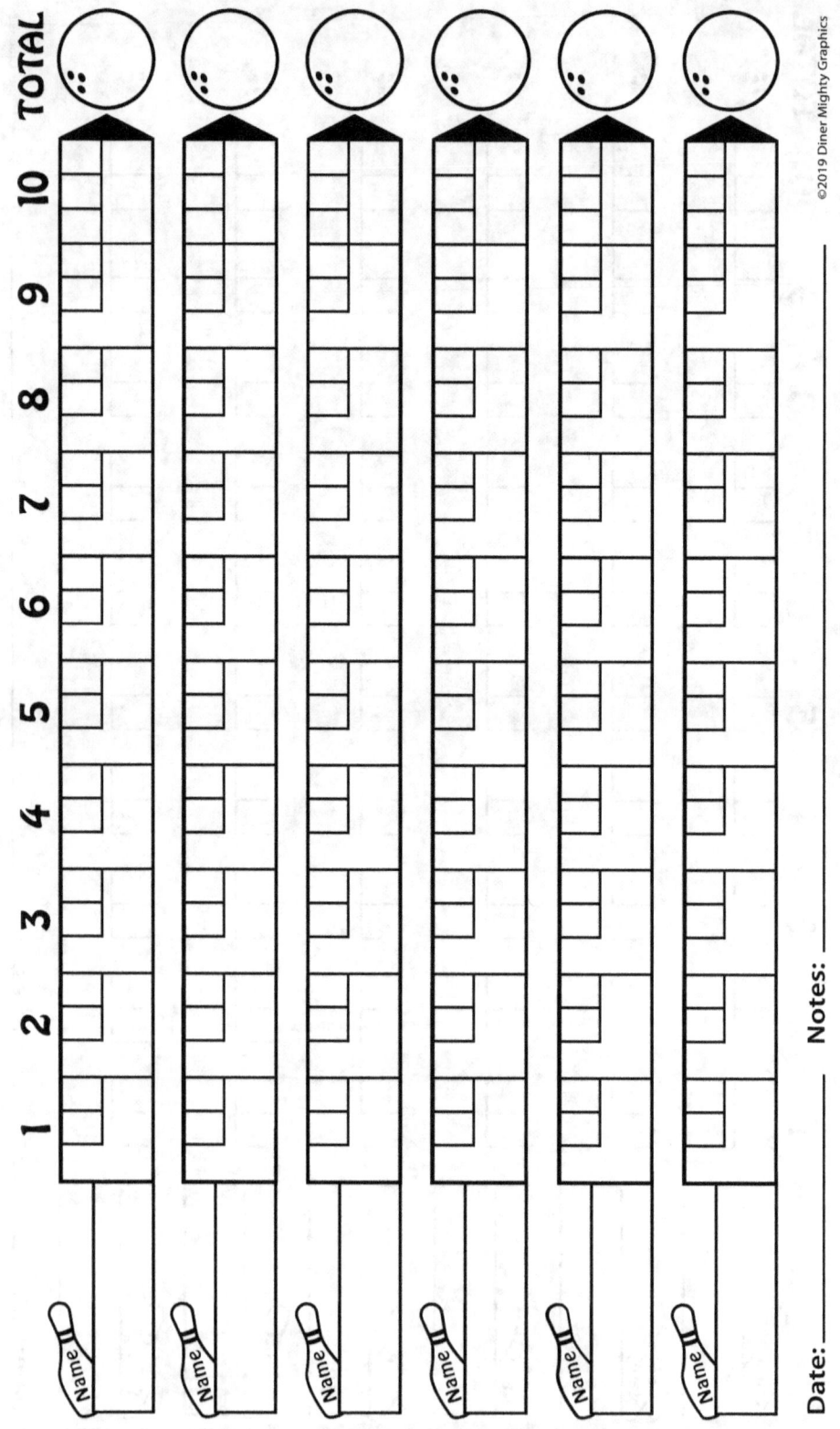

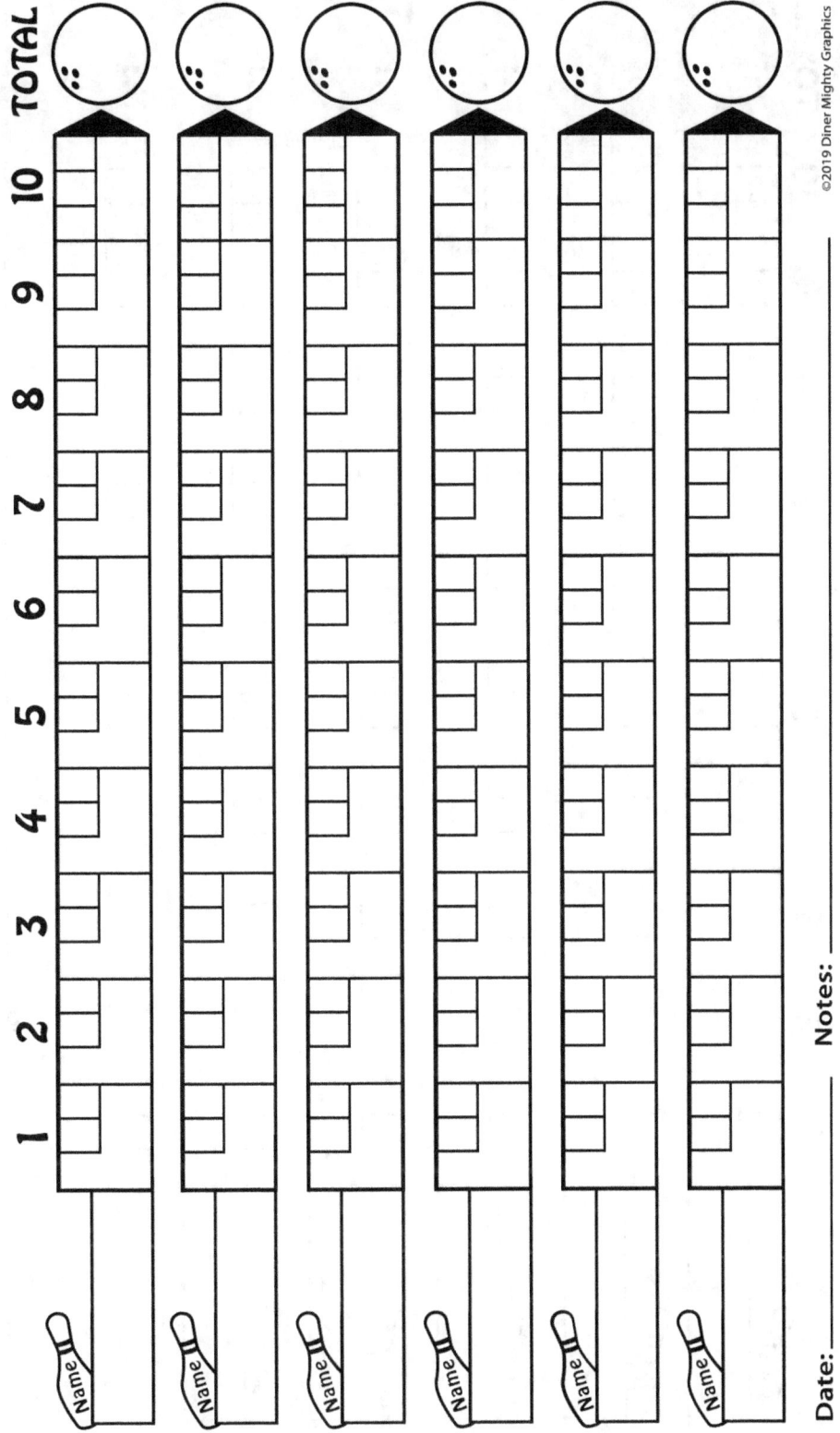

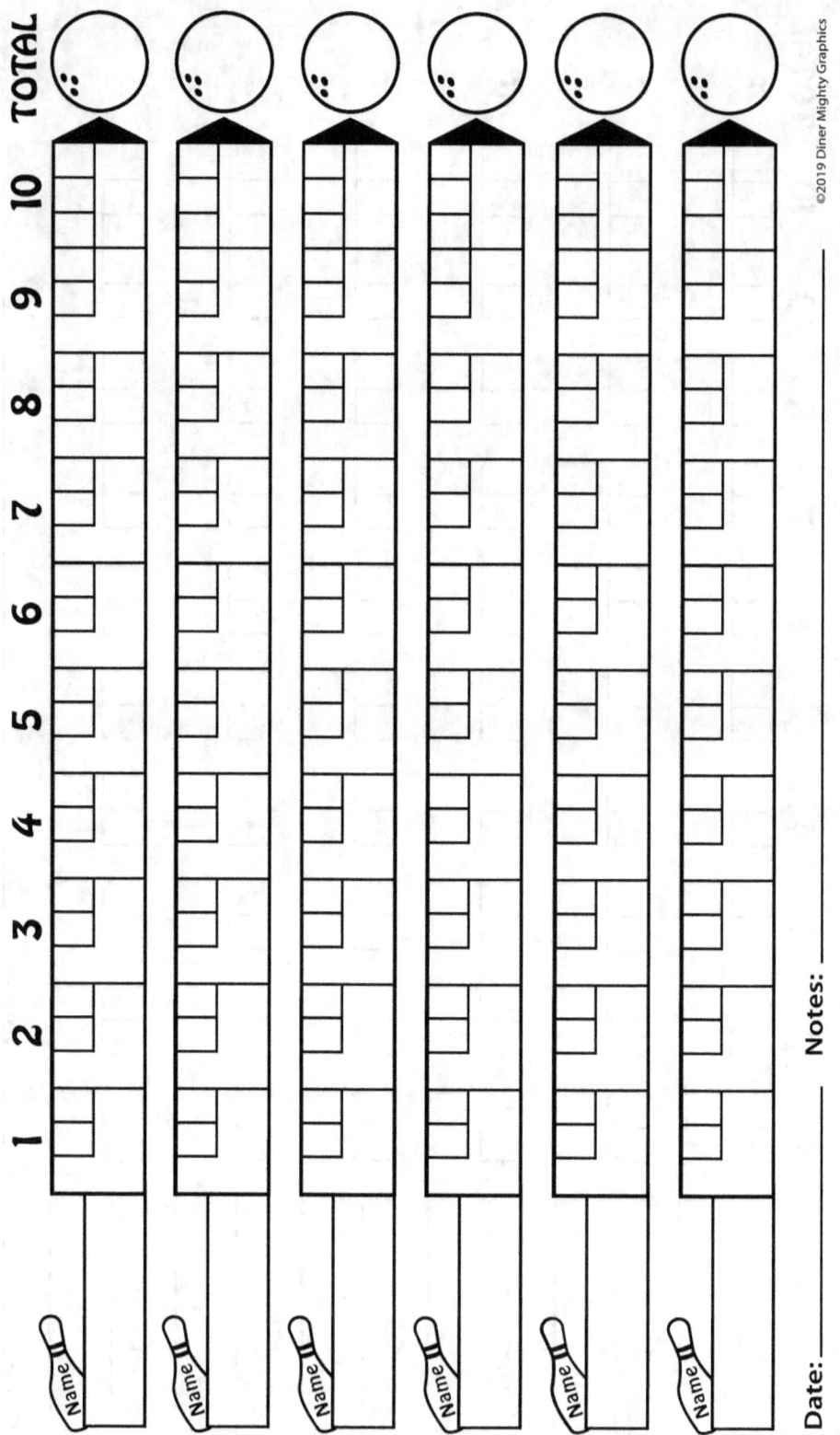

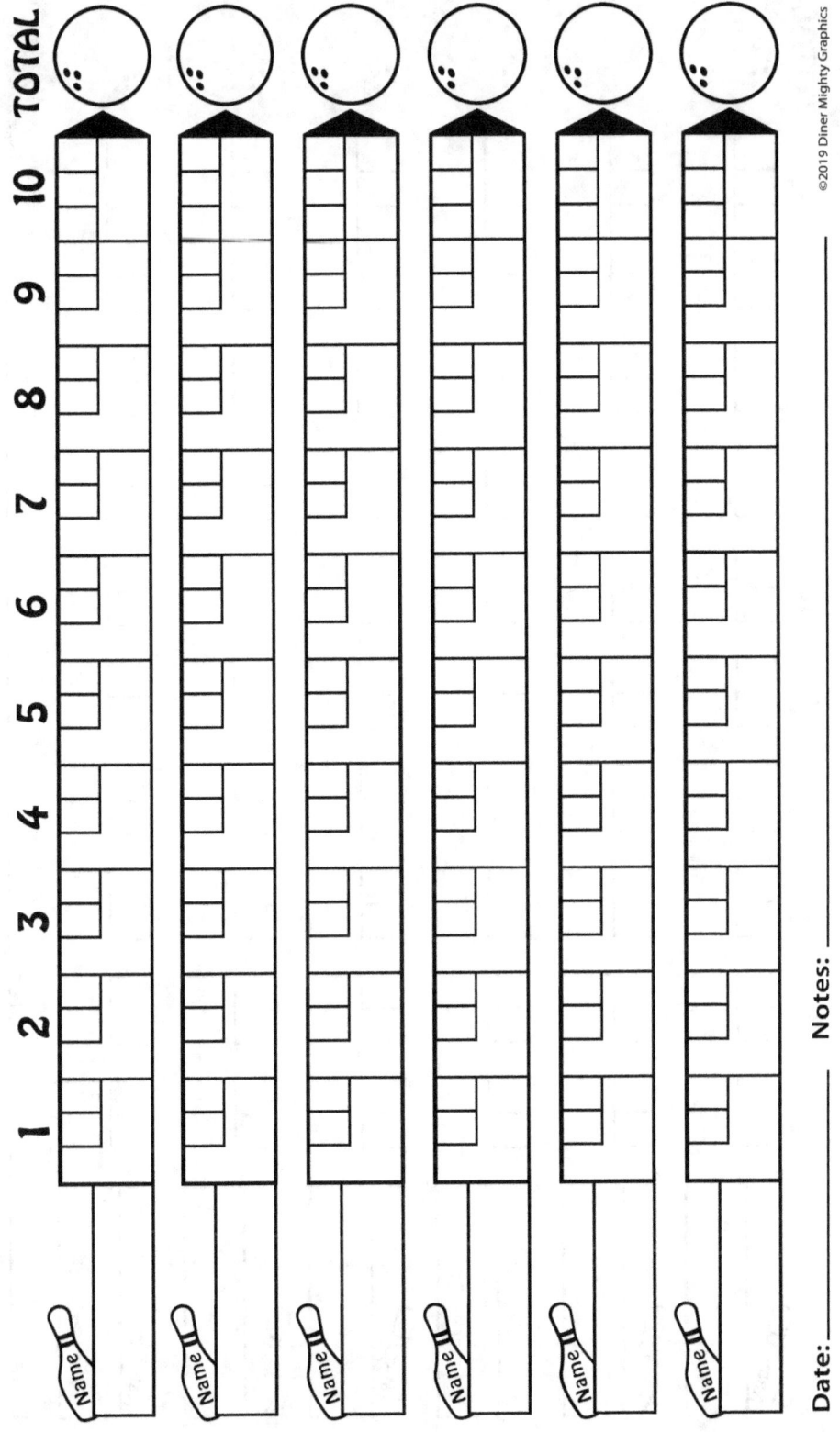

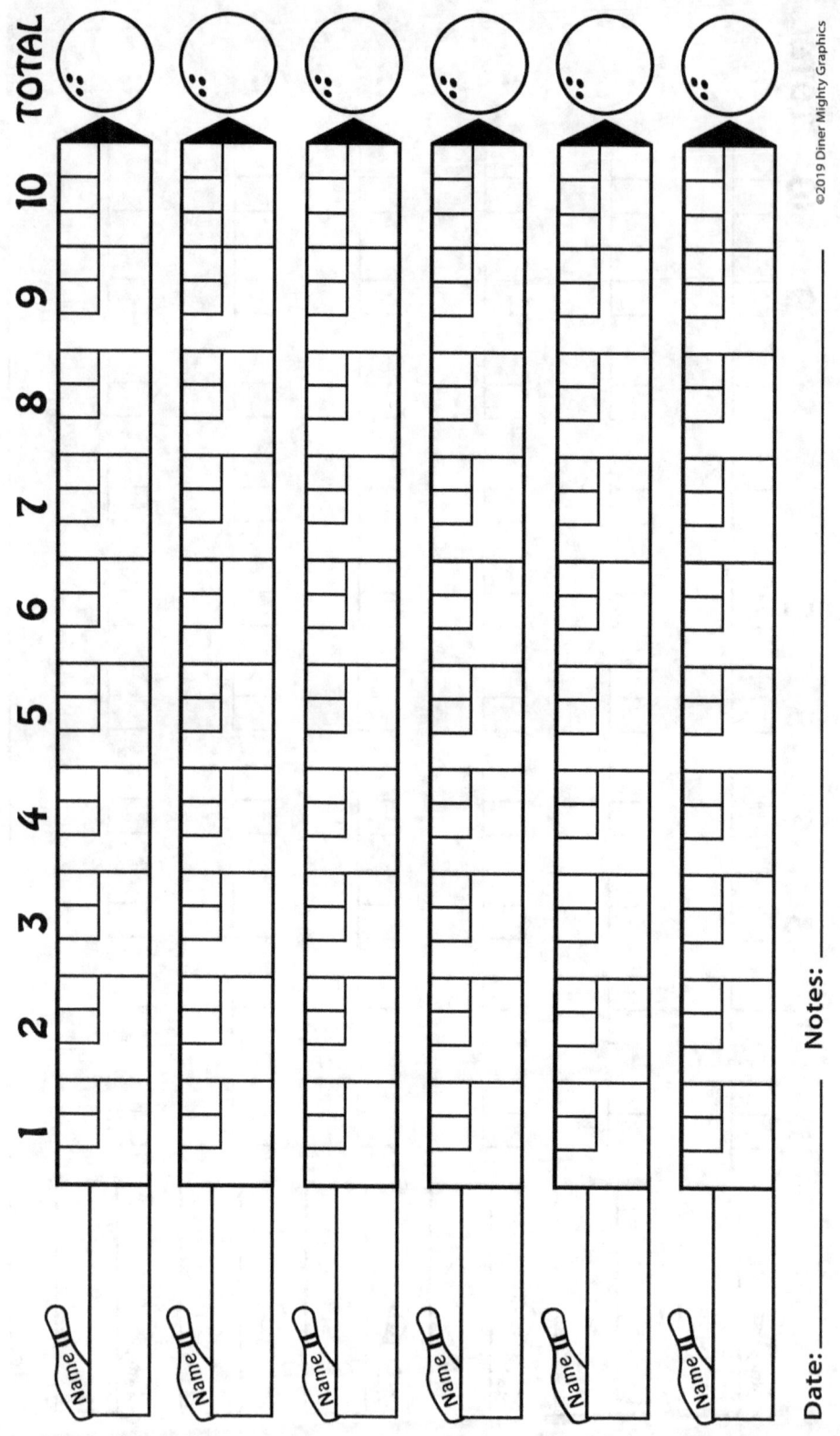

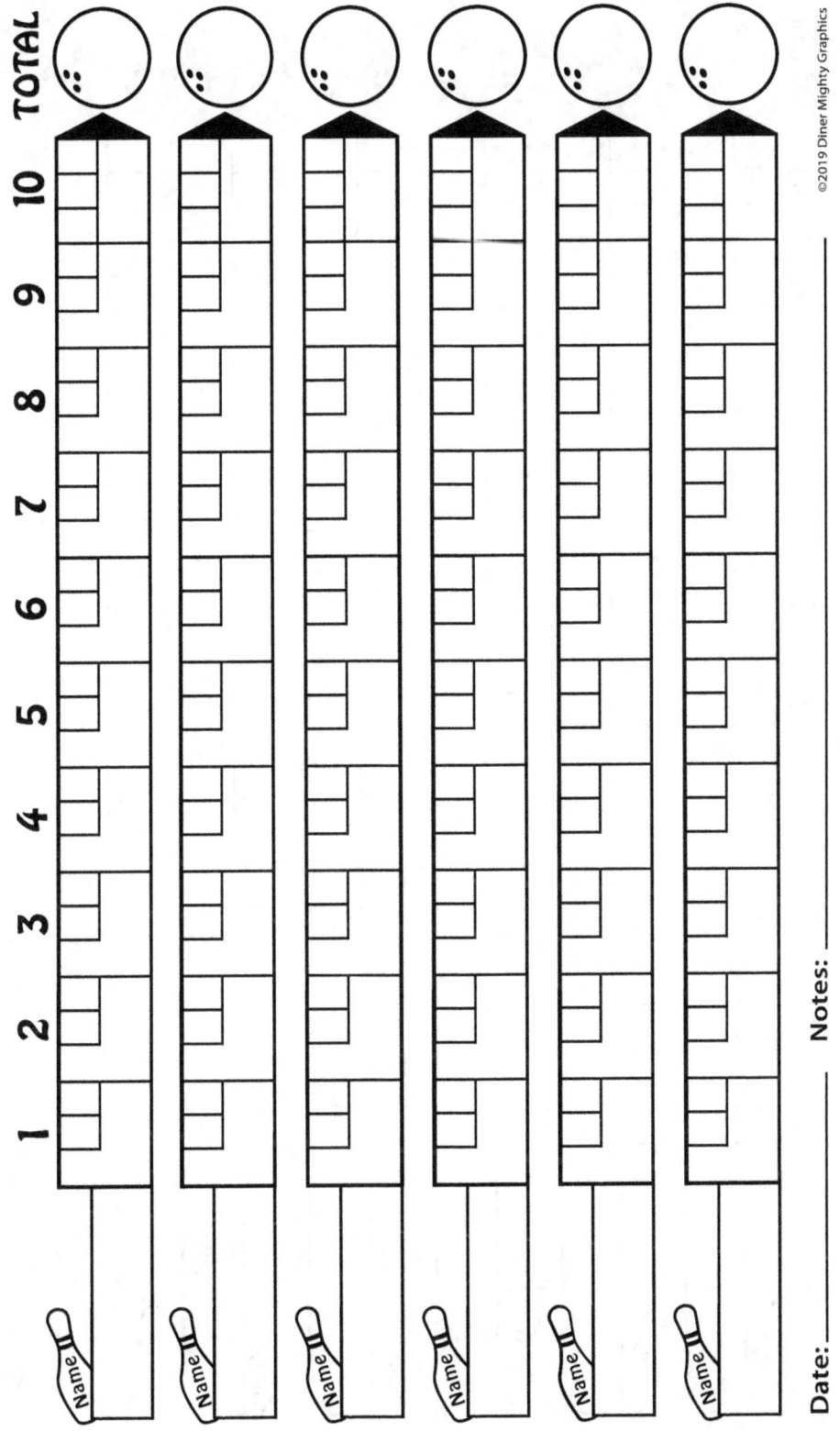

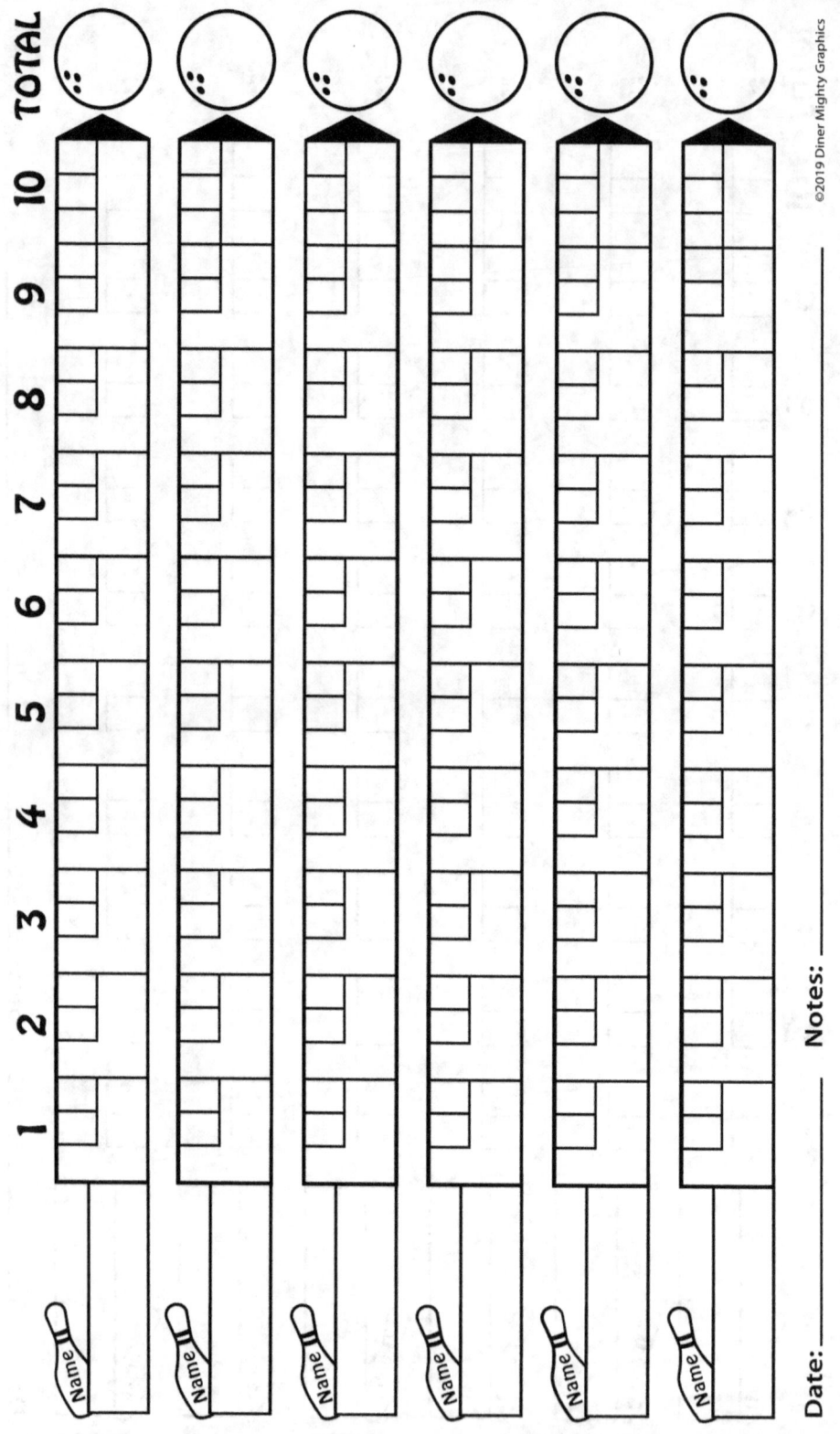

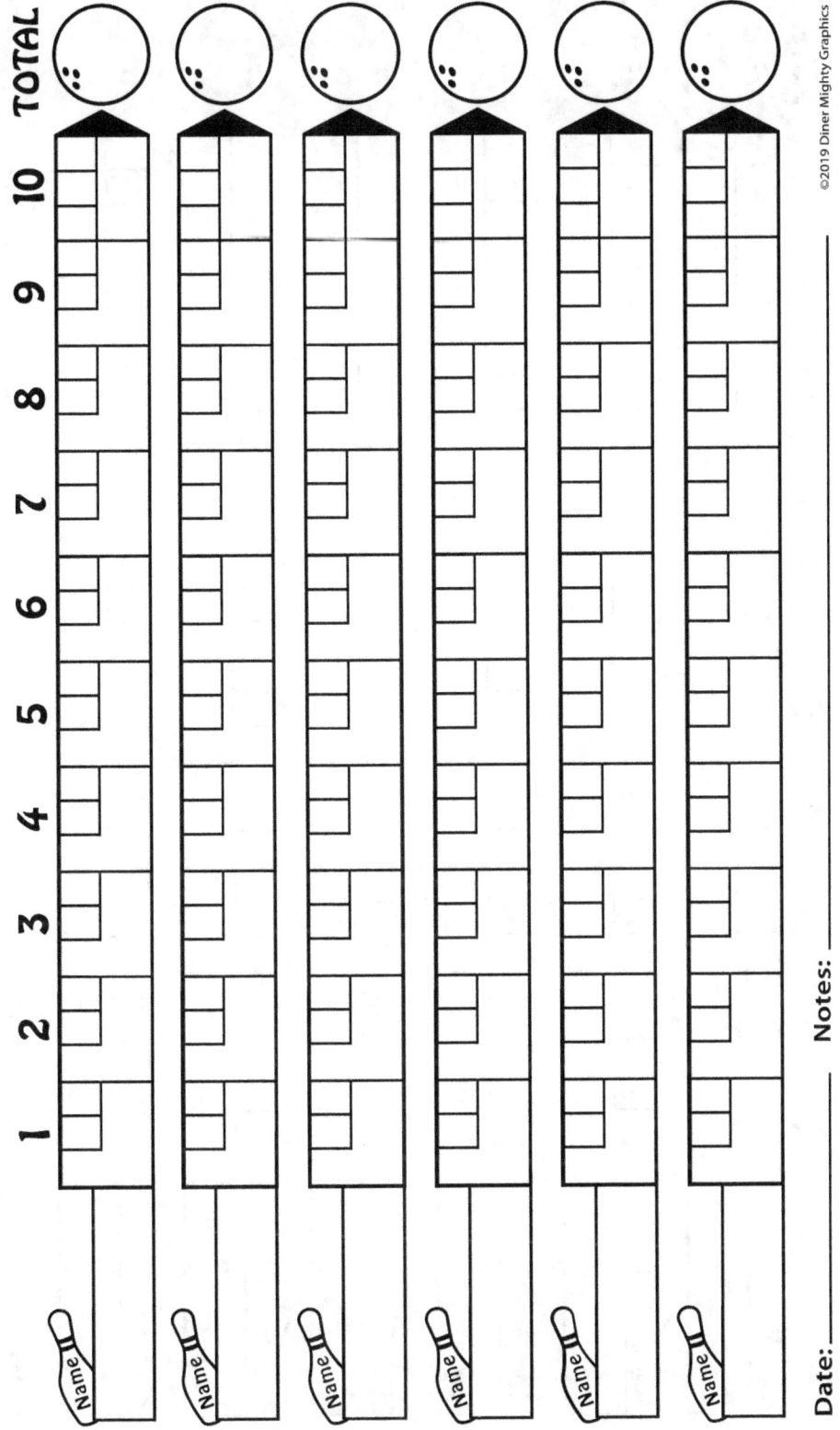

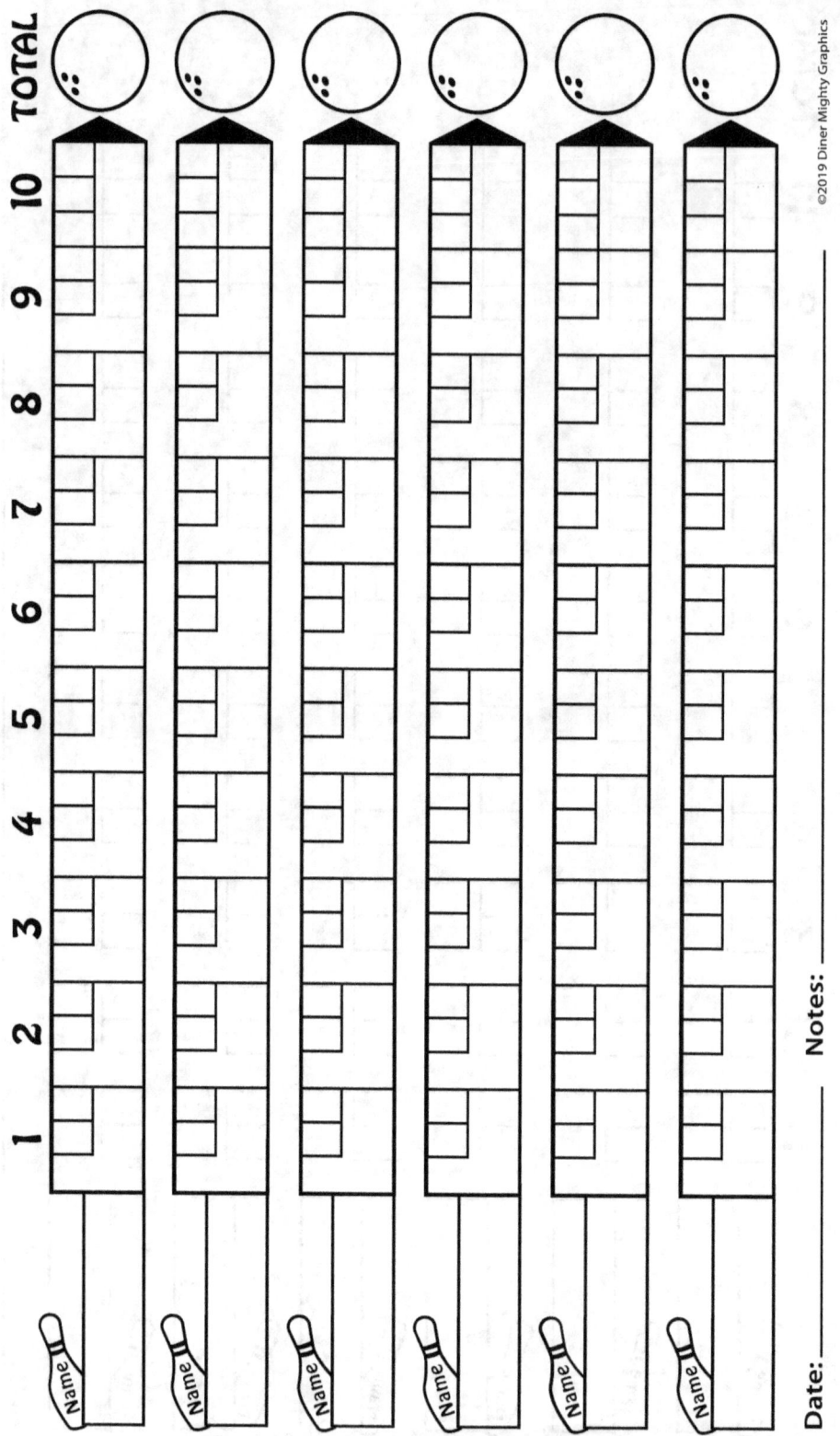

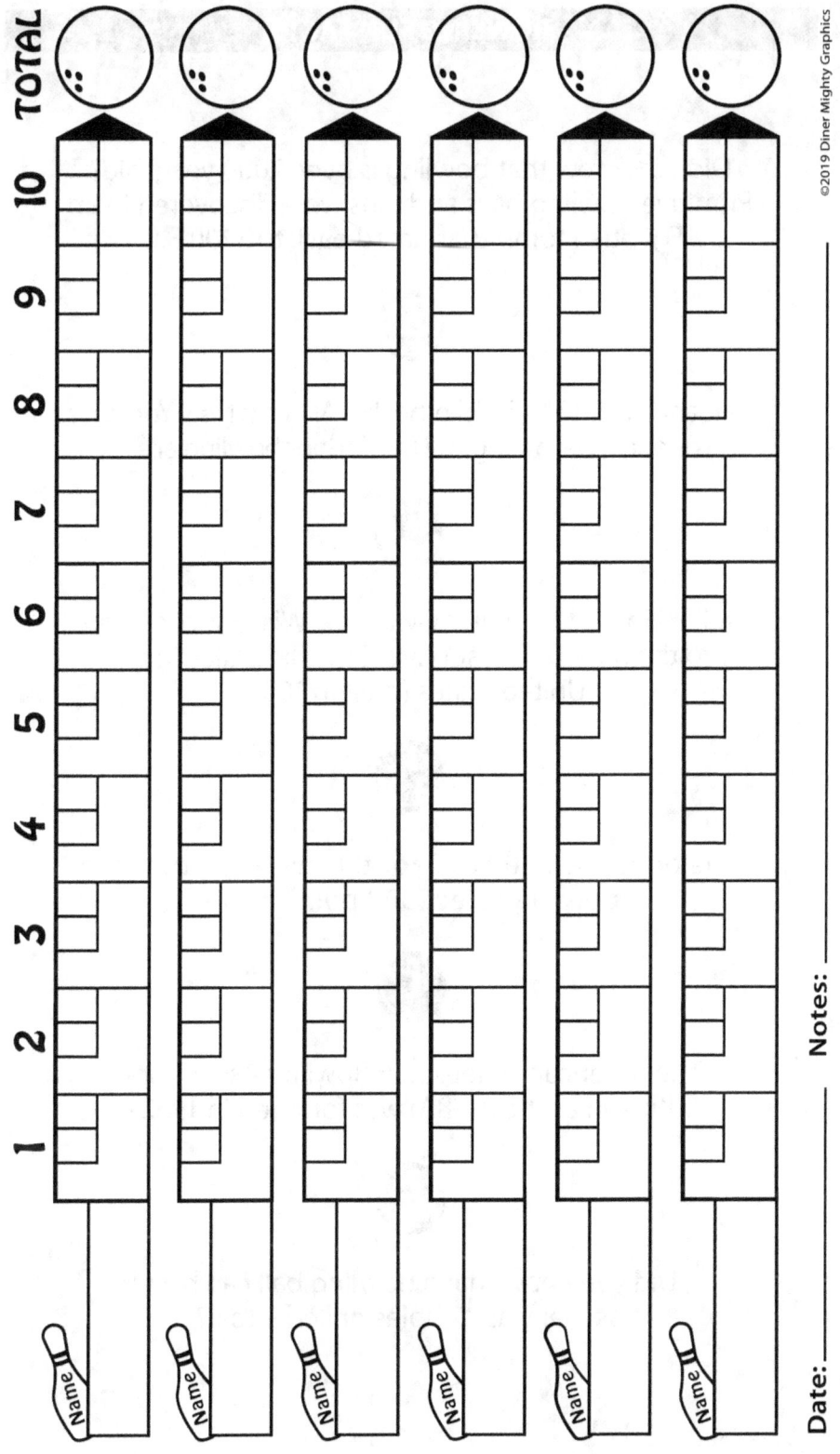

BOWLING FUN FACTS

Did you know that bowling is over 5,000 years old? Primitive bowling balls and pins were discovered in an Egyptian tomb that dated back to 3200 B.C.

On January 1, 1840, Knickerbocker Alleys in New York City opened, becoming the first indoor bowling alley.

Holler House tavern in Milwaukee, Wisconsin is home to the now-oldest surviving bowling alley in the United States (built in 1908).

The odds are 1,500 to 1 for the average bowler to bowl a perfect 300 point game.

The American Wheelchair Bowling Association (Known as the AWBA) was founded in 1962.

Did you know that a bowling ball can have as many as 12 holes drilled into it?

In the early 1900s, bowling balls were made of wood.

The first women's bowling tournament took place in 1917 in St. Louis, Missouri.

The largest bowling alley in the world is in Japan. It was built in 1972 and has 116 lanes and can accommodate up to 696 bowlers.

Bowling pins can last up to three seasons of league playing. After that, they need to be replaced.

Before the electronic pinsetter was invented in 1936, young boys were hired to roll the balls back to the bowlers and pick up and reposition the bowling pins for the next roll of each frame.

The computerized scoring system (known as an automatic scorer) was first introduced into bowling alleys in the 1970s.

Did you know that the White House has a bowling alley? It's one lane and is located in the basement.

What pirate has the best curve ball?
CAPTAIN HOOK!

Why didn't the bowling pins show up for the big game?
THEY WERE ON STRIKE!

Which reptile is the best bowler?
THE ALLEY-GATOR!

Why do cars enjoy bowling so much?
THEY LIKE THE LANES!

There was a bowling ball that got arrested.
IT WAS FRAMED!

What did the banana say to the ice cream after bowling?
LET'S SPLIT!

Why did the bowling chicken cross the road?
TO GET TO THE OTHER LANE!

A hot dog bowled a perfect game.
HE WAS ON A ROLL!

Did you hear about the pilgrim who liked to bowl?
HE GOT A THANKSGIVING TURKEY!

Why was the puppy asked to leave the bowling alley?
HE KEPT FETCHING THE BALLS!

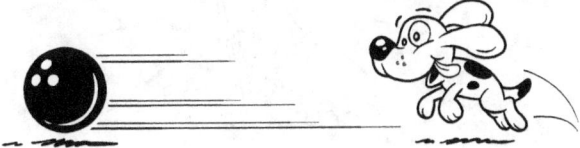

Why do bowling balls like to live in Hollywood?
THEY ALWAYS GET THE BEST ROLLS!

Why are chickens such bad bowlers?
THEY ALWAYS FOUL!

A bowling ball didn't have enough postage.
HE GOT RETURNED!

What happened when the bowling pins heard this joke?
THEY FELL OVER LAUGHING!

Who is the leader of the bowling alley?
THE KING PIN!

The team's score was so pretty. You know what they did?
THEY PUT IT IN A FRAME!

Some bowling pins went to a party.
THEY HAD A BALL!

Why are raindrops such bad bowlers?
THEY ALWAYS ROLL INTO THE GUTTER!

Why do lions like bowling so much?
THEY'RE ALLEY-CATS!

Why don't balloons like to bowl?
THEY'RE AFRAID OF THE PINS!

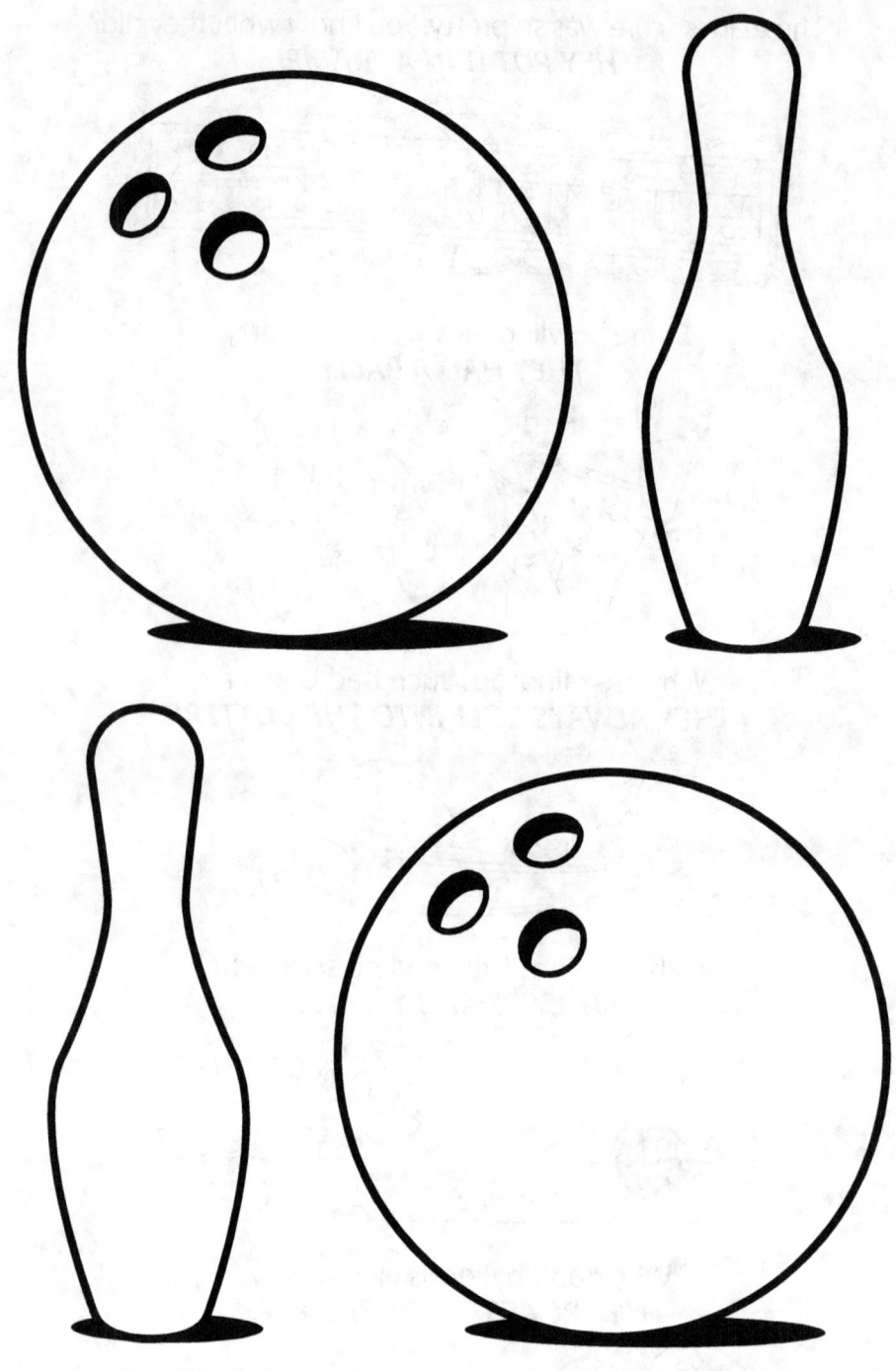

If you could design your own custom bowling balls and pins, what would they look like? Use a pencil or crayon to draw some fun designs!

WORD SEARCH

```
R W A L L S H O T E E T
C P T G U T T E R K N U
R B P L R I E B L I O R
O R O L L P G A P R B L
F K C W T M K G D T M Y
R E K D L R N G F S A D
G T E S P I I E B U H O
Y G T G K W N R K O T U
E K C F R A U G W E M B
K H O O K A R A B M S L
R E T S M I X E R A P E
U O G S P I N N E R L F
T R O L N L K E G F I L
G V T S E S I G L E T R
S T R H E R A P S C O A
```

PIT	GUTTER	FRAME	BOWLING BALL
STRIKE	SPLIT	DOUBLE	TURKEY
ROLL	KEGLER	KINGPIN	MIXER
BAGGER	WALL SHOT	GRIP	POCKET
HOOK	SPINNER	HAMBONE	SPARE

WORD SCRAMBLE

Unscramble the letters below to reveal four bowling words.

M A E F R
☐ ☐ ◯ ☐ ☐

P I G R
☐ ◯ ☐ ◯

L I T S P
◯ ☐ ☐ ☐ ☐

T E G U R T
☐ ☐ ☐ ☐ ◯ ☐

Did you hear about the bowling ball who got a flat tire?

Place the letters from the circles here:

◯ ◯ ◯ ◯ ◯

Unscramble the letters to get the answer to the cartoon riddle!

EVERYTHING TURNED OUT OK— HE HAD A ◯◯◯◯◯ !

FIND THE THREE BOWLING PINS THAT ARE THE SAME

DRAW ALLEY GATOR

Using a pencil or crayon, match the numbers in the boxes below to draw a picture of Alley Gator™!

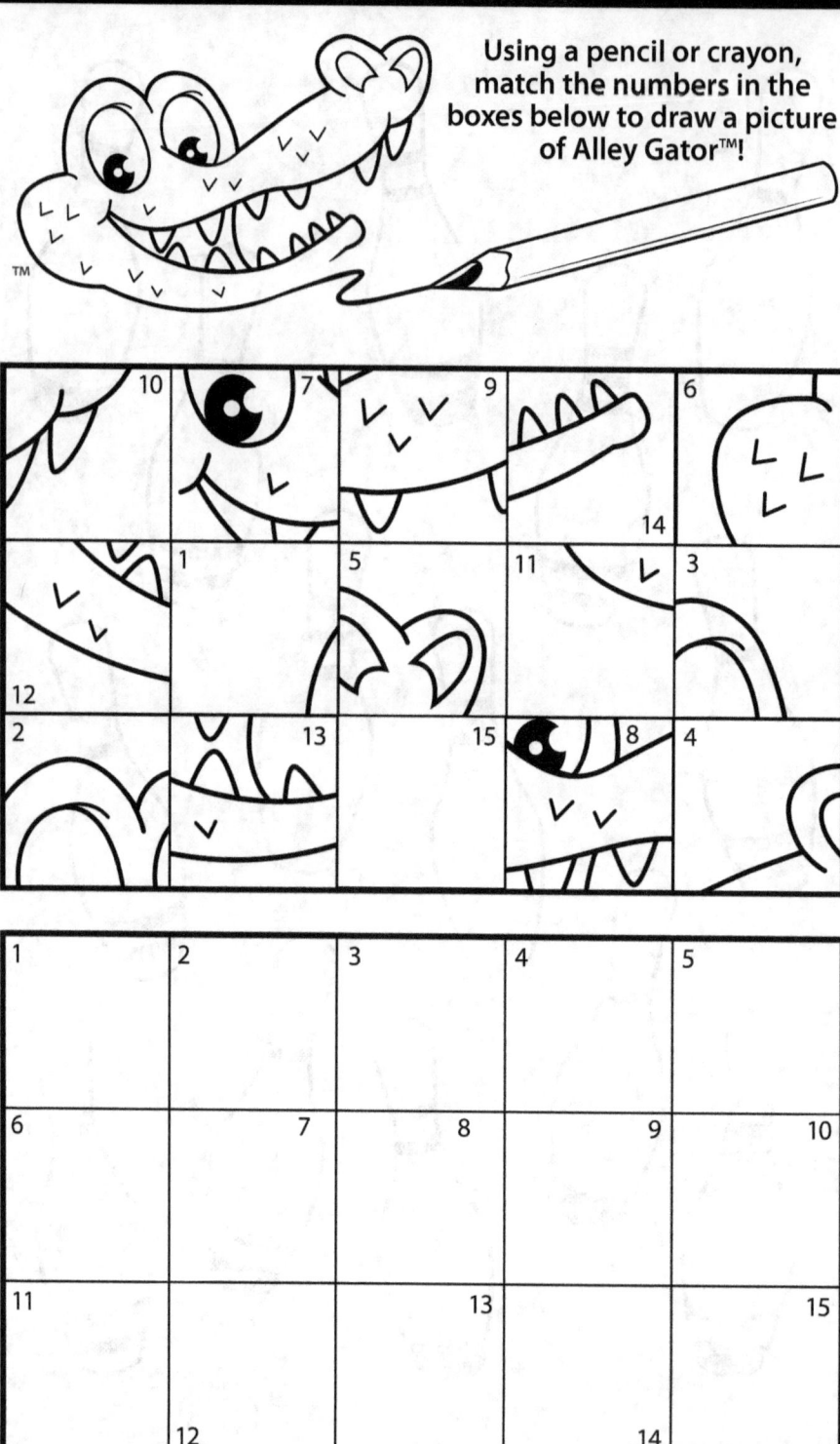

BOWLING QUIZ

1. Three strikes in a row is called a _____.

2. The channel is another name for the _____.

3. The maximum weight for a bowling ball is _____ pounds.

4. The wood used to make bowling pins is _____.

5. A bowling lane is _____ feet long.

6. A perfect game is a score of _____.

7. The name given to a person who bowls is _____.

8. What is the name of the inside middle pin? _____

9. Duckpins are tall and thin. True or False?

10. How many boards make up a bowling lane? _____

11. A bowling ball can have as many as _____ holes drilled in it.

12. The ideal place to hit the pins is called the _____.

13. Candlepin bowling balls have no holes. True or False?

14. Two strikes in a row is called a _____.

15. A _____ is when all 10 pins are knocked down on the first roll.

16. How many frames are in one game of bowling?

17. Ten-pin is the most common form of bowling. True or False?

18. The area behind the pin deck is called the _____.

19. The way you hold a bowling ball is called the _____.

20. A circle around a number indicates a spare. True or False?

ANSWERS

WORDS SEARCH

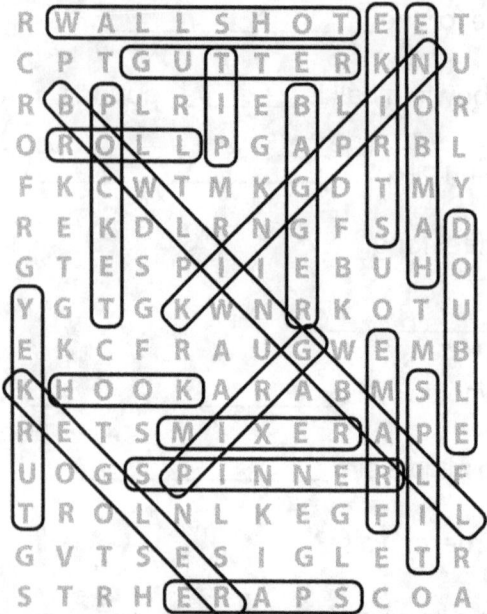

BOWLING QUIZ

1. Turkey
2. Gutter
3. 16
4. Rock maple
5. 60
6. 300
7. Kegler
8. King pin
9. False
10. 39
11. 12
12. Pocket
13. True
14. Double
15. Strike
16. 10
17. True
18. Pit
19. Grip
20. False

WORD SCRAMBLE

M A E F R
F **R** **Ⓐ** **M** **E**

P I G R
G **Ⓡ** **I** **P**

L I T S P
S **P** **L** **I** **T**

T E G U R T
G **U** **Ⓣ** **T** **E** **R**

A R P S E
S **P** **Ⓐ** **R** **E**

BOWLING PINS

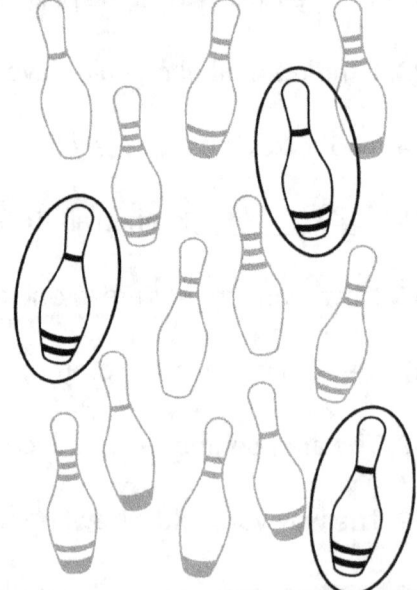

www.ingramcontent.com/pod-product-compliance
Lightning Source LLC
Chambersburg PA
CBHW071915070526
44583CB00016B/2007